AMERICA'S YESTERDAY

THE PALENQUE BEAU RELIEF
(Courtesy of the Field Museum, Chicago)

AMERICA'S YESTERDAY

BY

F. MARTIN BROWN

PROFUSELY ILLUSTRATED
WITH HALF-TONES AND
LINE ENGRAVINGS

PHILADELPHIA

J. B. LIPPINCOTT COMPANY

LONDON

CONTENTS

5

ILLUSTRATIONS

7

AMERICA'S YESTERDAY

CHAPTER ONE

MAN OF ANTIQUITY

1

AN eminent divine of two centuries ago, the Reverend Dr. Lightfoot, made an exhaustive study of the genealogy of man as set forth in the Old Testament and came to the conclusion that Adam was created at 9 o'clock in the morning of October 4th, 4004 B. C. There are doubtless people who today believe in so literal a translation of the Bible that Dr. Lightfoot's date for the advent of man is acceptable to them. There are others, however, who disagree and place man's beginning hundreds of thousands of years ago. That they do this does not mean that they are irreligious to any degree at all. They have examined the evidence and found that it does not agree with the facts that have been discovered through the patient toil of scientists.

The most ancient evidences of man's predecessors that might be considered human to any degree are the fragments of a skeleton or several of them discovered at the beginning of the century by Dr. Du Bois near the little town of Trinil in Java. These are the upper portion of a skull, several teeth and a thigh bone. These bones are so different from those of modern man that some argue that they really represent an extinct great ape. It seems, however, from the structure of the entire bone and of the teeth that the remains represent a creature more nearly man than ape. The reconstructions from the hands of competent men such as Sir Arthur Keith and Dr. William Gregory are probably fairly representative of what the Java ape-man looked like. His carriage was slightly stooped with flexed knees and a single sweeping curve in the back. The heavy bony ridges above the eyes, the low flat nose and protruding mouth show a distinct relationship to the apes, but the volume of the brain cavity, especially its fore part, and the structure of the teeth are much more closely related to those of man. Just how old these remains are in terms of years is nearly impossible to say and actually immaterial. The river deposit in which they were found is ancient, the oldest in which the remains of the ancestors of man have come to light. The old world predecessors of our own ancestors have been so frequently and so well discussed elsewhere that I shall not take the space to repeat it here.*

The period of time, geologically speaking, during which man lived in America is the only one to which I shall devote any space in discussing man's occupancy of Europe. All prehistory is the study of the development of man's culture and in Europe, especially in France, the sequence through which he has passed is thoroughly

---

* In the appendix, the reader will find a half dozen or more books that cover this field of man's history thoroughly.

known. All our American studies of man's progress must
be made with these fundamentals of European prehistory well in mind if we are to appreciate fully Ancient
Man here.

The earliest type of Stone Age inhabitants of which
any considerable amount of remains has been discovered is the Neanderthal species of man that has been
named *Homo neanderthalensis*. This species of man
lived in most of Europe at about the beginning of the
last series of glacial advances and retreats. That he was
not present during the previous geological period, the
Pliocene, seems to be a fairly well-established fact.
None of his remains, either skeletal or cultural, have
been found associated with the extinct animals which
mark that period. Before he arrived, from goodness
knows where, at least in Europe the Sabre-tooth tiger,
the Etruscan rhinoceros, the giant beaver and many others had disappeared. Many of the animals that are found
associated with the Neanderthal man are closely related
to species that exist today in the forests and fields of
modern Europe. There are, however, a number that
would surprise any modern hunter in France if he were
to come upon them. Elephants, mammoths, lions, broad-
nosed rhinoceros, spotted hyenas and hippopotami
roamed the land and give us ample indication of the
mild winters and generally warm, temperate climate of
Europe in the days when England and Ireland were a
part of the mainland and man began his long climb to
civilization.

These early men of Europe are considered a different species from modern man because of several striking differences in their structure. The crania are a curious combination of ape-like and man-like forms. A heavy ridge of bone circles the eyes, the forehead is low and the mouth quite jutting. Measurements show that in Europe as in America the earliest human occupants had long, narrow skulls. Like the Java ape-man, the man of Neanderthal could not stand erect. From the structure of the knee joint and the angle at which the thigh bone meets the pelvis, it is quite evident that his posture was markedly stooped and the knees constantly slightly bent. A distinctly ape-like character is found in the disproportionate relationship between the lengths of the upper and lower leg and of the upper and lower arm. In both cases the upper portion is noticeably shorter than the lower. From the vertebrae that have been discovered, it is evident that this species of man had but a single curve in his back, whereas modern, erect-standing man has a backbone with an S curve. They were a race of short people and probably did not average over five feet, five inches in height. From casts taken of the inside of skulls it has been determined that the brain of the Neanderthal man falls in volume within the range of that of modern man. It was not so highly developed, particularly in the frontal portion and in those characters of superior organization found in recent man. However, the bilaterally asymmetric development indicating one-handedness is found and is an important human character. That portion of the brain which is associated with the powers of speech is really poorly developed and it is supposed that the linguistic ability of these peoples was poor.

Apparently it was during the existence of the Neanderthal man that fire was conquered and turned to use. The evidence of hearths and camp fires places this somewhere near the middle of the period of his occupancy of Europe. His implements of hunt were probably at first only the crudest of stone weapons. As the race aged, he developed a fine technique in stone work and before the close of his era was capable of making very efficient tools both in stone and in bone. Just what caused the disappearance of the Neanderthals we do not know but apparently 20,000 or 25,000 years ago the first race of modern man entered Europe, probably from central Asia, and not long afterward *Homo neanderthalensis* was no more. No traces of pure Neanderthal type have been found in any of the upper paleolithic burial sites, nor does there seem to be the slightest trace of a people remaining bearing the Neanderthal cranial characters. Dr. Hrdlicka, however, holds the opposite opinion and feels that the Neanderthal man contributed in some measure to the makeup of modern man and that traces of his blood might be found even today in some parts of Europe. It seems that for a short time during the fourth glaciation the two species of man competed for the supremacy of Europe and the more brainy, better developed Cro-Magnon race of modern man won.

The new occupants of Europe were much larger than even the men of today and there is every evidence that they had more than proportionately larger brains. As a matter of fact, the Cro-Magnon woman seems to have surpassed the average male of today in that respect. In very few characters do they differ physcially from the men of today. There were no marked ridges of bone

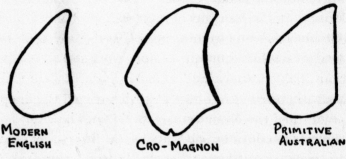

MODERN
ENGLISH

CRO - MAGNON

PRIMITIVE
AUSTRALIAN

MIDSECTIONS OF TIBIA (After Kieth)

about the eyes, the forehead was high and well developed, the nose narrow and aquiline, the cheek bones high and broad and the stature erect. One of the striking differences from the man of today is the shape of the shin bone which among the Cro-Magnon in cross-section is flat and long, while in recent modern man this section is markedly triangular. It is possible that in one or two communities of southern France and northern Spain and among the primitive inhabitants of the Canary Islands we have remnants of this, the first known race of our species. That this early form of our ancestors was extremely capable is readily seen in their unusually

fine workmanship in stone, their exquisite bone work
and their strikingly modernistic painting as it may be
seen today upon the walls
of caves in the Pyrenees.
It is among these people
that we first find any indication of reverence for
the dead and possibly a
belief in a life hereafter.
Ornaments, weapons and
food are found frequently
with their burials. Ap-
parently their love for
color or possibly the
preparation for the life
to come led them to
powder or paint the de-
ceased completely with
red ochre before burial.

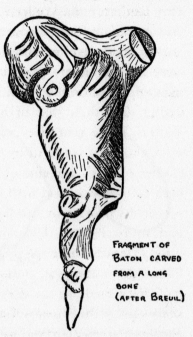

FRAGMENT OF
BATON CARVED
FROM A LONG
BONE
(AFTER BREUIL)

This pigment has stained many of the burial offerings
and bones that have been recovered from the graves of
the Cro-Magnon man.

2

Man's history in America dates back to the Ice Age.
How long before that time he roamed this continent we
do not know. In Europe there have been found the
evidences of several totally different species of man that
succeeded one another until modern man arrived. All

the evidences that have been accumulated concerning prehistoric man in America point to no species other than modern man. We have no Piltdown man, no Heidelberg man and no Neanderthal man as yet represented among the skeletal remains found in ancient deposits in America. For many years it has seemed that modern man appeared on this continent at what is probably an earlier date than that of his appearance in the Old World. These tentative conclusions have been based upon the ideas set forth by the paleontologists in their studies of fossil remains of other mammals that have been found associated with those of man. However, by recent discoveries we are led to believe that the early periods ascribed to those long extinct animals are not quite so far distant in the past history of the New World. Throughout the past, numerous finds of man's bones have been made in the gravels laid down thousands of years ago by the streams that flowed from beneath the glaciers that once covered almost all of Canada and many of our more northern states.

Probably the oldest find of this kind is a fragment of a human pelvis discovered in the upper terrace of the Mississippi River at Natchez. There is nothing about it to indicate that it belonged to a man of other than modern type. However, it was found in the same deposit with the bones of two different ground-sloths, *Mylodon* and *Megalonyx*. Upon examination by Dr. Thomas Wilson of the National Museum some time after the find, it was discovered that the human fragment was in an even

more advanced state of fossilization than the sloth bones
and consequently might be even older than they. Just
how old these bones are it is impossible to say in terms
of years. Geologists believe that the deposits in which
they were found belong to those laid down by the first
melting of the glaciers during the Pleistocene period. It
seems more likely, however, that the bones are not so
old as that. If we were to take the geologists' time estimate of this formation, something like 100,000 years,
we would have to consider that for probably 98,000 years
man made little or no advance in culture. From the history of man in Europe, where it is fairly well known
during his formative years, this does not seem possible.

For a long time it was suspected that the human fragment may have strayed into the deposit by some unknown means and thus have become associated with the
ground-sloth bones. That man in America knew and
hunted these clumsy beasts we now have ample evidence.
In 1929, Dr. M. R. Harrington of the Southwest Museum in Los Angeles, California, began excavating at
Gypsum Cave, Nevada, not far to the north and west of
Boulder Dam on the Colorado River. During the course
of three years' work at that one site, he produced evidence that cannot be contested that man was a resident
in these United States long before the ground-sloths
became extinct. Just how long ago that occurred we are
not very certain. Some intimation, however, of how recently these curious animals roamed in our desert southwest may be had from the fact that within the last two

decades a completely desiccated specimen was found. Two men from El Paso, Texas, exploring the small volcanic cones northwest of Las Cruces, New Mexico, entered a side passage to one of them where it opened into the throat of the main gas vent. There they discovered a complete, dried-out ground-sloth in practically perfect condition. For some time it stood against the wall in an El Paso garage and now may be seen in the Museum at Yale University. From this you may see that the task of stating in years how long man has been in America is a difficult one. There have been twenty-five or thirty discoveries of modern man associated with extinct animals in the United States alone. Before dating can be done with any certainty, much more must be learned of how recently the prehistoric animals became extinct.

In South America too, the remains of modern man have been found abundantly associated with extinct animals. In the early part of the last century a Danish explorer, P. W. Lund, searching for the remains of extinct mammals, examined over 800 caves. In six of these he found skeletal remains of man. Probably his two most interesting caves were at Lagoa Santa in Brazil. There he collected human bones and one stone utensil along with great quantities of remains of extinct mammals. The cave was situated on the borders of a lake which, in the rainy season, overflowed into it. At the time of his exploration, during the dry season, the floor was dry and under the thin layer of black earth he discovered bones in various states of fossilization. Some

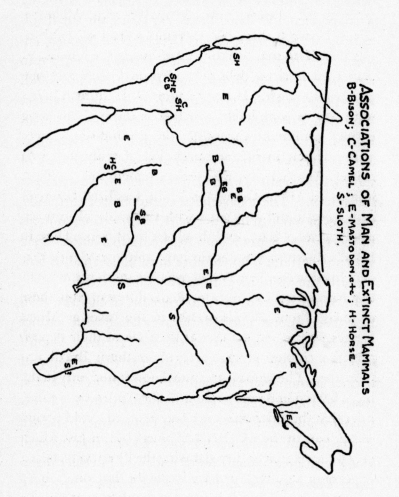

ASSOCIATIONS OF MAN AND EXTINCT MAMMALS
B-Bison; C-Camel; E-Mastodon.etc.; H-Horse
S-Sloth.

were quite fragile, light in color and in weight and others were very heavy, hard and dark brown. All intergrades between these two extremes were found mixed together. This makes it difficult to assign the remains of man to a horizon definitely identified with any one group of the fossils. However, some of the human bones were just as completely petrified as those of the long extinct mammals. Curiously, the ground-sloths were quite evident in this accumulation of truly fossilized matter. Another cave that was extremely interesting is located in Minas Geraes. In it the fossilized bones of man were found associated with the bones of four extinct species of llama and those of a fossil horse. Here in Lund's discoveries we again have ample evidence that man lived in the New World at a time when the animals that roamed its fields were markedly different from those of today. From the discoveries in the caves at Minas Geraes we can assume that at the time of their deposition the climate of that area of southern Brazil was quite cool. The llama is an animal now found only in the high, barren and cold regions of the Andes. So we may infer that these deposits were laid down in a cold period during one of the six glacial advances but in just which one of the six that occurred during the Pleistocene epoch we cannot say. It may have been the last one, about 12,000 years ago, but it is more probable that it was the second one from the last, in the neighborhood of 25,000 years ago.

Turning again to North America, we find that evi-

dences of man have been found on the great western
plains at Folsom, New Mexico, associated with a long-
extinct species of bison, a tremendous
beast much larger than the species we
know today, with large, flat, broad horns.
The find in this case was not the bones
of man but his handiwork. There were
among the bones of these buried fossil
skeletons of the extinct bison a number
of flint points that had been used probably on *atlatl* darts. These points are of a
very distinctive type and well worked. The
most typical characters are a longitudinal
groove flaked from the base to nearly the
point on both sides and they are wider
near the tip than at the base. They lack

FOLSOM POINT

stem, shank or side notches of any description. These
and points similar to them have been designated Folsom points.

Dr. Frank Roberts has described this find and the
trouble to which the archeologist must go to establish the
evidence of antiquity for such discoveries in America so
clearly that I quote him verbatim from *Smithsonian
Miscellaneous Collections* XCIV, no. 4, 1935, pp. 3–6:

"Because of a certain amount of confusion and mis-
understanding concerning the original Folsom finds, a
brief review of the subject is germane to the present
discussion. In the summer of 1925 Fred J. Howarth and
Carl Schwachheim of Raton, N. Mex., both now de-

ceased, notified Director J. D. Figgins of the Colorado Museum of Natural History, Denver, of a bone deposit which they had found in the bank of an arroyo on the upper sources of the Cimarron River near the town of Folsom in eastern New Mexico. Samples of bone sent to the museum indicated that the remains were those of an extinct species of bison and of a large deerlike member of the *Cervidae*. Prospects for fossil material were so promising that the Colorado Museum sent a party to the site in the summer of 1926. During the course of the excavations, carried on under the supervision of Frank Figgins and Mr. Schwachheim, parts of two finely chipped projectile points were recovered from the loose dirt at the diggings. Near the place where one of them had been dislodged a small, triangular piece of 'flint' was found embedded in the clay surrounding an animal bone. This fragment was left in the block of earth, and when the latter was received in the laboratory at Denver, the dirt was carefully cleaned away from the bit of stone. It appeared to be from the same material as one of the points, and close examination showed that it actually was a part of the point. This evidence seemed unquestionably to demonstrate that here was a definite association between man-made objects and an extinct bison.

"Director Figgins was so impressed with the find and was so thoroughly convinced that it was of importance to students of American archeology that he took the points with him that winter when he visited several of the large eastern museums on paleontologic business.

In most places his announcement was courteously yet skeptically received. One authority on stone implements marveled at the quality of workmanship that the specimens exhibited and even remarked that they were reminiscent of the finest examples from Western Europe. He was doubtful, though, of the trustworthiness of the association. He thought that it could perhaps be attributed to an accidental mixing of material. Others said that the points had no significance because they could be duplicated in existing collections. At a few museums, notably the American Museum of Natural History, Mr. Figgins was urged to continue the work in the hope that additional evidence could be obtained.

"The Colorado Museum again sent a party to Folsom in the summer of 1927 and had the good fortune to find additional points. One of these was noted before it was removed from the matrix, even before it was completely uncovered. Work was stopped immediately on that part of the excavation, and telegrams were dispatched to various museums and institutions inviting them to send representatives to view the point in situ. The writer at that time was attending the first Southwestern Archeological Conference at Pecos, N. Mex., and, upon receiving notice of the find and travel instructions from Washington, proceeded to Folsom. Arriving at the fossil pit, on September 2, he found Director Figgins, several members of the Colorado Museum board, and Dr. Barnum Brown, of the American Museum of Natural History, New York, on the ground. The point, which became the pattern and furnished the name for the type, had just been uncovered by Dr. Brown. There was no question but that here was the evidence of an authentic association. The point was still embedded in the matrix between two of the ribs of the animal skeleton. In fact it has never been removed from the block, which is now on exhibit in the Colorado Museum at Denver. On returning to Raton, N. Mex., that evening, the writer telegraphed to Dr. A. V. Kidder at Pecos and urged that he visit the site. Dr. Kidder arrived 2 days later, and he and the writer drove out to the bison quarry. After the whole situation had been carefully studied, it was agreed that the association could not be questioned. Furthermore, it was ascertained that the points were totally different from the ordinary types scattered over that portion of the Southwest.

"At the meeting of the American Anthropological Association held at Andover, Mass., in December of that year Dr. Barnum Brown and the writer reported on the Folsom finds. There was considerable discussion of the subject, and although many agreed that the discoveries were important, there was still a general feeling of doubt. Numerous explanations were offered to show that the points might have gotten into such an association without actually being contemporaneous with the bison remains. Several mentioned that points of that type were numerous in collections from certain mound sites, from village sites in New York State, and elsewhere, and for that reason they could not be very old. Others insisted that, although they accepted the conclusions on the genuineness of the finds, there must be some mistake about the antiquity of the animal remains.

"The summer of 1928 saw the American Museum of Natural History and the Colorado Museum cooperating at the Folsom site. The expedition was under the leadership of Dr. Barnum Brown, who was assisted by several graduate students in anthropology. The latter were under the general supervision of Dr. Clark Wissler. Additional points and bison skeletons were found, and telegrams reporting the discoveries were sent to various institutions. This time numerous specialists—archeologists, paleontologists, and geologists—rushed to see the evidence. The consensus of the informal conference held at the site was that this constituted the most important contribution yet made to American archeology. Some of the most skeptical critics of the year before became enthusiastic converts. The Folsom find was accepted as a reliable indication that man was present in the Southwest at an earlier period than was previously supposed."

During 1931 near Carlsbad, New Mexico, a similar spear point was found directly associated with extinct bison and musk ox. Again, the association with musk ox indicates man's presence on the American continent during a cold period, a period of glacial advance. It was not until the summer of 1934, however, that any discovery was made of the men who made these easily recognizable flint points.

During July a Mr. Jensen discovered in gravel hauled from a near-by pit in Brown's Valley, Minnesota, an artifact resembling the Folsom type. His curiosity being aroused, he investigated the pit and found several others and in addition a few human bones. He communicated with Dr. Jenks of the University of Minnesota who investigated the find and brought to light the burial of a Folsom point maker.* This skeleton resembles in many respects that of an American Indian. It differs, however, in several items. The breadth of the jaw is tremendous, greater even than the extraordinary width of the jaw of the old man of Heidelberg. The facial proportions seem to eliminate the possibility of its being an Eskimo. Curiously, the breadth of the head is greatest in the occipital region at the base of the skull, a character found today among some of the most primitive peoples of Patagonia and not uncommon among the skulls recovered from the Brazilian caves by Lund. This skull shows many characters in common with that of the Magdalenian Chancelade man of France.

Fortunately, geologists had not long finished a thorough study of the gravel formations in Minnesota. According to them the gravel in which the Brown's Valley man was interred dated from the time of the Tinta period of Lake Agassiz. This lake occupied the area

---

* The term is here used in a broad sense. Dr. Roberts thinks that the Minnesota man may have been a local variety but surely is not a true Folsom point maker.

wherein Lake Winnipeg and the Wisconsin lakes are now found. At that time the great ice sheet had clogged the present outlet of the lakes and Lake Agassiz drained through the Mississippi Valley. The gravels in which the burial was found were deeply overlaid by a deposit put down during the last great period of melting, before the lakes as we know them today were formed. It is estimated that this occurred from 10,000 to 12,000 years ago. It is curious to note that at this time man in Europe was practicing what is commonly termed the "red ochre" burials and that the Brown's Valley man, too, represents a "red ochre" burial.

All this indicates that modern man lived in America well back into the glacial epoch. However, the Brown's Valley man is the only one that gives us a reasonably accurate idea of the time of his existence. Dr. Barnum Brown of the American Museum of Natural History has estimated that the Folsom deposit is fully 20,000 years old. Whether this is true will depend upon the results of further study and more extensive exploration of the fossil fauna of America. Harrington, in his admirable paper on the finds at Gypsum Cave, has summarized the association of man with extinct mammals. He lists fourteen species including horses, camels, bison, ground-sloths, mastodons and mammoths that have been associated definitely with man and twenty-one others for which we have some evidence of an association. Man has been living on these continents for a long, long time.

3

The most enduring remains of very early man are the stone tools he fashioned and used. In general these are classified according to the technique by which they were made. The names used are all derived from the typical locality in France where they were discovered during the study of man's advance in Europe. Since this system is satisfactory, it is generally applied to the stone artifacts associated with primitive man throughout the world. The earliest of these are called eoliths since they appear at the dawn of man's use of stone. It is difficult to say just what characterizes a true eolith. So many stones are found that may or may not have been used by man that only those which definitely show the effects of hammering or pecking are usually admitted. These first stone tools were nothing more than conveniently shaped fragments of stone or handily rounded pebbles picked up, used a few times and thrown away. They have been found associated in England with the Piltdown man and are the type of stone tools that were used by the most primitive natives of Australia at the time of its discovery by Europeans.

EOLITH FROM NEAR PILTDOWN (After Dawson)

The earliest step in the development of true tools on the part of man is called Chellean because of its discovery at Chelles, France. These have been made from various pieces of flint or chalcedony that, with little work, could be shaped into crude but serviceable tools. The shaping was done by striking a glancing blow at the edge which caused thick, short flakes of the material to

CHELLEAN COUP-DE-POING FROM ST. ACHEUL (From spec. in A.M.N.H.)

ACHEULEAN COUP-DE-POING (After Osborn)

spawl off. None of these Chellean artifacts is symmetrically shaped. The flaking along the edge is crude, unsymmetrical and ragged. They are the meanest type of stone scrapers, knives, awls and hand hammers that have been found. Gradually the Neanderthal man improved his technique and hammered the stone into symmetrical forms, making artifacts that show flaking over their entire surfaces. Such implements were found first at St. Acheul and are called Acheulean. Both surfaces of the working edge of this class of implements have been retouched by percussion. Occasionally small scrapers were made by this method from the flakes struck from the larger and more clumsy tools. The next step in the development of stone work was found at La Moustier. The Mousterian implements were made almost entirely from large flakes. The big, clumsy hammer stones and

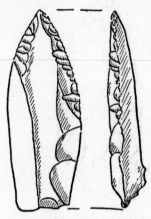

MOUSTERIAN POINT

coup-de-poing were no longer held in favor. All sorts of implements were made from these flakes struck from flint nodules. In general, however, they were worked or shaped on one side only. The workmanship differs markedly from anything that preceded it. The forms are quite symmetrical and the retouching along the edge is well done. The tiny spawls that have been struck off are narrow and long. This was the highest state of development in the art of flint making as we know it before the advent of modern man.

The earliest Cro-Magnon men in Europe first manufactured stone tools that differ but little from the Mousterian type. In general the implements of this, the Aurignacian period, are made from long, slender flakes. There is still only one side retouched and the artifacts are little different from the Mousterian. However, this forerunner of modern man soon developed the finest stonework that has ever been found. Because of its abun-

dance at Solutré this type is called Solutrean. There
seems to have been a complete revolution in the method
of retouching the flint edge. In the previous types the
flaking was done by striking sharp blows
that flaked off slivers of the stone. In the
Solutrean artifacts the retouching was done
by means of pressure. After the flint had
been shaped roughly it was held in the
hand, pressed with all four fingers against
a piece of leather which protected the
palm. A pointed piece of stone, bone or possibly very hard wood was set firmly against
the edge to be retouched and with a quick
downward pressure a long, slender flake
stripped back from the implement. By this
method it was possible to take very slender
and thin flakes of flint and work them into
knives or points of great beauty. On many
of the finest pieces these pressure flakes
have spawled off halfway across the tool.

SOLUTREAN
POINT (After
de Mortil-
let)

The modern Indians who use the same method for
shaping arrow points and scrapers start at the point and
work toward the base as they quickly fashion the instrument. A good craftsman can shape and finish an arrow
point in about thirty minutes.

In Europe from the time of the Solutrean industries,
workmanship in stone degenerated while workmanship
in bone developed. In America at least some of the peo-

ple approached and equaled the finest of Solutrean stonework and seem to have been at that point in cultural development at the time of the discovery of this continent by Europeans.

CHAPTER TWO

THE BASKET-MAKERS

1

OF the early peoples who lived in America we have not enough information to enable us to say much about their life. As a matter of fact, it is only of those who have lived here since the beginning of the Christian era that we have any appreciable information. The earliest in either cultural or chronological sequence are the Basket-Makers. This group of people developed in the Southwest and lived there at least as late as the middle of the 8th century. How much later they were to be found on the American continent is difficult to say but there is reason to believe that they were still living in caves or near them as late as the 10th century. They were not the ancestors of the Pueblo people who are now living in the arid part of our country. Not only was their culture quite different but their physical makeup differed from that of the Indians who were met by the invading whites. As their name signifies, these people were preëminently adept at basketry. From their era onward to the close of American prehistory at the opening of the 16th century the archeologists have unraveled the mystery of the Southwest.

The earliest people were simple, primitive agriculturalists probably not far removed from a nomadic
state. Although their cultural period is divided into
three eras, Basket-Maker I, II and III, it is only of
Basket-Maker II and III that we can speak. The first
step in their development is the hypothetical forerunner that must have occurred antedating the Basket-
Maker remains that have been found. Basket-Maker II
people, for the most part, lived in caves. It is very doubtful that they built any shelters whatever. Some instances
have been observed of semisubterranean cists larger
than ordinary that may have been used as houses during
particularly inclement weather. The later Basket-
Makers built houses that seem to have evolved from their
grain storage bins. These are partly under ground where
the earth walls are held in place by means of vertical
slabs of rock. The superstructure seems to have been
made of poles supported along a ridge and covered with
dirt and sod. In the roof over the center of this circular
or semicircular house, there was a hole for light and the
exit of smoke. Around the walls are occasionally found
crude bins dug into the earth. At the height of the development of this type of domicile, the main room was
augmented by a narrow, low passage dug into the ground
to a vestibule. It is probable that these openings were
covered with skins or mats to reduce the draft.

The Basket-Makers of all stages made characteristic
burials in either abandoned rock-lined storage cists or
in similar pits dug into the hardpan of the cave floor.

A BASKET-MAKER CAVE

VIEW FROM A BASKET-MAKER CAVE
Photos. by the Author
Penrose-Taylor Expedition to Yampa Canyon, Colorado

Often more than one body was interred in such burials. Possibly to reduce the labor and also to prevent the spirit of the deceased from haunting or doing damage, the bodies were trussed up, the knees drawn to the chest, before burial. From these funeral pits a sufficient number of skeletons have been recovered to give us an idea of the stature and physical conformation of these people. They were moderately tall, broad-shouldered and well-set-up. Their heads were of the type called dolichocephalic. This merely means that the head was rather narrow for its length, the breadth being less than 70% of the greatest length. There are no indications of deformation of the skull being practiced by these people. Thus they seem to be of a stock totally different from the round-headed Pueblo people who supplanted them.

Like all very primitive agriculturalists, the Basket-Makers cultivated very few plants and probably depended upon hunting for the larger portion of their food during the summer season, storing grain to carry them through the less productive months of winter. The early Basket-Makers had, so far as we know, only one staple plant product, a hard, yellow, flint corn that does not seem to be grown today by any of the Indians. Toward the close of their period there appeared the common bean that is so important in the diet of the Southwest and Mexico. How many centuries ago the culture of maize or, as we call it in this country, corn was introduced into the Southwest it is difficult to say. We know that it came from Mexico and probably from the

Valley of Mexico. I suppose it would be conservative to state that at least 1200 years were necessary for the development of this food plant from its supposed progenitor, *teocintli* grass. That would make the beginnings of corn culture in America earlier than 1000 B. C. and if it spread slowly probably as early as 2000 B. C.

The people we are discussing had, at least during the latter part of their era, one domestic animal, the dog. Several partially mummified remains of this friend of mankind have been found, but one of the most startling evidences is a pair of beautifully woven belts found by Dr. Earl Morris in a Basket-Maker cave just across the New Mexico line in northern Arizona in 1929 or 1930. I had the pleasure of determining the source of the hair that had been used to make the wool for these belts and it proved to be that of a short-haired dog.

The clothing worn was scant—in the summertime probably nothing more than a coarsely woven breech-cloth or apron and in the winter crudely fashioned robes of rabbit fur. The feet were protected from the hot sands and rocky country by woven sandals. The shape, method of tying and weave of these is characteristic of the Basket-Makers. They are always square-toed, with a tie cord made of hair between the great toe and the one next to it leading back and around the ankle and down to the heel. Some of these sandals are crudely made of split yucca leaves while others are finely fabricated from twisted cedar bark and other plant fibers. Those showing the highly developed workmanship are usually re-

EARLY BASKET-MAKER STORAGE CIST
Note Corn-cobs on Stone at Left

LATE TYPE BASKET-MAKER STORAGE CIST
Note Corn-cobs at Bottom
Photos. by the Author
Penrose-Taylor Expedition to Yampa Canyon, Colorado

enforced on the bottom and this reënforcement covers
the entire sole. Sandals plaited of whole yucca leaves are
not associated with these people nor are the sandals of
the side-loop type. Tie strings of plant fibers are not
found. All cord and string made by the Basket-Makers
is of hair. The use of cotton and Apocynum fiber was
introduced by a later people.

Several types of fabric were manufactured by these
cave dwelling people. Cloth woven of fur twined with
plant fibers is not uncommon. Bags of varying sizes and
small pieces of cloth were made of twined cords. From
the fragments of cloth that have been recovered it is evident that the loom played no part in their manufacture.
Toward the close of the Basket-Maker period the fur
cloth was replaced by one in which downy feathers were
caught in the string and used for the weaving. It is also
among the later Basket-Maker remains that we find any
extensive use of matting, usually made from tule grass
and Apocynum string. The presence of this plant fiber
string is an indication of the decadence of the true
Basket-Maker culture.

The infants of these primitive people were carried
about on crudely constructed but very well padded cradles. The body of the cradle was made of short, straight
willow branches and the padding of bundles of either
fine grass or soft, shredded cedar bark. Just how these
cradles were carried we don't know.

Apparently the Basket-Makers were fond of ornaments. Numbers of grinding stones have been found

that were used to prepare colored pigments for bodily decoration. A great many strings of beads, some of small snail shells, some of acorn cups, others of bits of bone and stone have come to light during the excavations. That these people used tobacco or some other plant for smoking we know from the characteristic squat clay pipes. These pipes are straight-stemmed and resemble bloated cigar holders.

The principal weapon of the Basket-Maker like that of his forerunner, the Nevada cave dweller, was the

A THROWING STICK AND DART

throwing spear or *atlatl*. This interesting weapon is still in use among some of the most primitive peoples of the world. It consists of three pieces. A short fore shaft frequently not over eight inches long tipped with a flint point fastened to it by means of sinews and pitch formed the distal end. This short shaft fitted snugly into a socket on the main shaft which was much longer, in some instances five feet long. The throwing stick proper had a notch in the end that fitted the heel of the main shaft. The opposite end of the throwing stick was held in the hand and the main shaft steadied along it with the thumb and forefinger. The weapon was thrown in a manner similar to that of the javelin of today. The throwing stick, however, was not released but retained in the hand. If the kill was not made on the first throw, the dart constituting the fore shaft and point remained imbedded in the beast and the long main shaft dropped out and could be recovered. Many of the fore shafts were patterned with intricate designs in color. This may have been done to identify them. The main shaft usually had several short bands of clipped feathers attached to its side to steady it in flight.

The basketry for which these people are so renowned varies from rather crude to extremely well-fashioned pieces. Twilled or plaited work is absent but a variety of coiled types is abundant. All manner of material of plant origin was used in this work and frequently large pieces were decorated with bits of fur. Not only were seed and food storage baskets of the usual shape formed, but also flat, shallow baskets probably for the drying of grain and large, slender-necked baskets entirely pitched within to be used for water bottles. The Indian basket maker used no tools other than a crude stone knife and awl. The many curved shapes were modeled over the various parts of the worker's body. The coiled technique which we see so abundant in the Basket-Maker deposits may be divided into ten different varieties based upon structural characteristics. In general these varieties depend upon the foundation around which the thin splints of wood are wrapped. Two principal types of foundation were used: solid rods formed from the soft stems of such plants as the willow and bundles of soft fibers from the leaves of yucca or the bark of cedar. One of the commonest forms is a combination of these two primary types made by alternating courses of rods and bundles. Thin strips of wood that had been softened by soaking in water were used to sew together these rods and bundles in such a manner that a firm basket was made.

Usually in the rod-and-bundle type the sewing strip passed around the rods and through the bundles of fibers, depending on the strength of these to hold the basket together. In the various types using just rods for a foundation, the stitches usually pass two or more of the rods in such a way that each successive course is bound to the upper rod of the course below it. A variation from this type of weaving is found when the actual sewing splints are interlocked in each loop. By using different kinds of wood or the same kind stained with plant juices, the basket maker could work into her product simple patterns.

The second generic type of basketry is the woven basket. In the simple form of this type materials of the same kind are used for the warp and weft and the resultant product has a fine checkerboard or twilled appearance. All manner of variation of this type of weaving is found among primitive peoples. Wicker work in which the warp is inflexible and the weft slender and flexible is very old indeed. Probably it is the oldest type of basketry known. Among peoples who have no other types, we do find the wicker basket. The transition from this to the checkerboard in which both strands are flexible

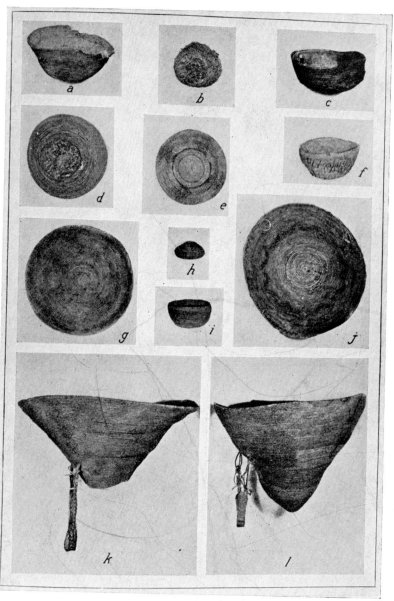

BASKET-MAKER BASKETRY
(Courtesy of Peabody Museum, Harvard University)

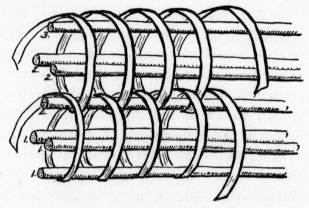

BASKETRY WITH THREE ROD FOUNDATION
(After Mason)

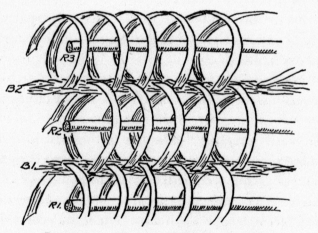

BASKETRY WITH ROD AND BUNDLE FOUNDATION

is easy and combinations of checker or twilled work with wicker work are not rare.

The matting that is sometimes found in Basket-Maker caves is usually made from tule or rush. I have seen, however, a sample from the Yampa Canyon that was formed by weaving together flattened rush stems with a cord made from yucca fibers. This made a mat that could be rolled up easily and tucked out of the way. It is impossible in so brief a volume as this to cover fully any of the crafts or cultures of primitive peoples. The bibliography in the Appendix contains references to several works devoted solely to basketry. Probably the best of these was written by Otis T. Mason and forms a part of the *United States National Museum Reports* for 1902.

Toward the end of the Basket-Maker period their basketry shows signs of deterioration and the earliest types of pottery begin to appear. Apparently this first pottery was made by lining a basket with clay and then burning away the basket. Such crude utensils were poor. They were extremely thick, would not hold water and were easily crumbled. The last of the Basket-Makers, however, seem to have improved and learned to form pottery by hand as it is still done in the Southwest. Their ware is characterized by its thin walls and occasional crude decoration, though most of it is undecorated. At sites which were occupied at the close of the period there have been found a few skeletons that differ from the true Basket-Makers in that the heads are brachy-

CHECKER AND TWILLED BASKETRY

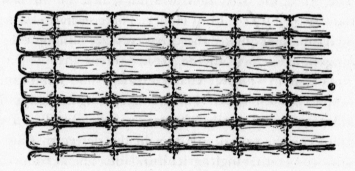

MATTING OF TULE AND YUCCA FIBER FROM YAMPA CANYON

cephalic or broad in relation to their length, indicating that the Pueblo type of Indian was beginning to infiltrate the region. Curiously these broad skulls show no evidence of the deformation that characterizes the true Pueblo Indians. It is just barely possible that these broad-heads introduced to the Basket-Makers true pottery and the bow and arrow which supplanted the basketry and the *atlatl*. Were these broad-heads the forerunners of the Pueblos?

2

In addition to the Basket-Maker culture there seem to have been two others that contributed largely to the succeeding Pueblo culture in the Southwest. One of these, the Hohokam, has been known for some time. The other, the Mogollon, was unearthed for the first time in 1933 by Dr. Emil Haury. There seems to be no direct relation among the three cultures although the Mogollon is closer to the Basket-Maker than to the Hohokam in cultural characteristics. The Hohokam people, like the Basket-Makers, were long-headed and did not practice skull deformation. They lived in the south central part of Arizona in the desert area and practiced a rather high agricultural life. Their extensive irrigation systems can be seen still, better from the air than from the ground. Their villages are characterized by rather large pit-houses with entrances on the side. These people were far in advance of their eastern and northern neighbors in the great variety of objects that they made. Their pottery was especially good for such an early time, around 800 A. D. In stone, bone and shell

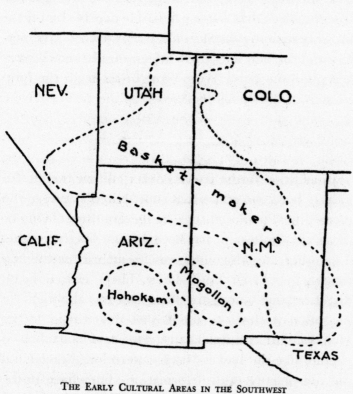

THE EARLY CULTURAL AREAS IN THE SOUTHWEST

they did highly decorative work, making many utensils such as awls and needles and a great many decorative necklaces and beads. A striking difference that is evidence of a distinct train of thought is their almost universal use of cremation for the disposal of the dead. The cultural remains of these people have much in common with those of the Archaic horizon in Mexico including what are considered early ball courts.

The Mogollon people who lived in southeastern Arizona and southwestern New Mexico in the region later occupied by the Mimbres pueblos were physically closer to the Pueblo people, being round-headed. They did not, however, practice deformation of the cranium. It is probably to be expected that the earliest of the round-headed people in the region would not do this since deformation appears only in moderately high primitive cultures. Their houses were like those of the Hohokam, side entrance pit-houses, and differed in that respect from those of the Basket-Makers. However, in practically all other respects they were more closely related to these latter people. Stone pipes, *atlatl* points, storage pits and flexed burials are found among the Mogollons and are characteristic of the Basket-Makers too. It is in pottery that these people show a greater advance in culture and through it they seem to be the link with the early Pueblo people. They had three kinds of ware: a plain ware, a dark brown ware and a red painted ware. Very little of it was decorated in any other manner than by scoring as with a bundle of twigs. It is possible that this brown-on-red ware is the predecessor of the much later Chihuahua and Mimbres potteries. Toward the close of the 9th century the true Pueblo peoples seem to have exercised considerable influence over them and head deformation and black-on-white pottery appeared. Dr. Haury states that the skeletal material indicates a close relationship between these people and those of the early agricultural settlements in the southwestern plains area—the Pawnees, Wichitas and Arikaras. Thus it seems that at least part of the advanced Pueblo culture came in from the east.

Whether it was these eastern migrants that brought the bow and arrow into the Southwest or a stream of people from the north and northwest is still unsettled. But the evidence of both weapons, the *atlatl* and the bow and arrow, being used by the Mogollons, at least during the latter part of their development, tends to indicate that toward the close their culture was a fusion of two. It is possible that the immigrants who developed the greater part of the Pueblo culture and who though round-headed differ from these earlier people in having much higher, vaulted skulls were responsible for the more effective weapon, the bow and arrow.

Four houses of the late phase have been dated by means of tree rings. They were erected between 896 and 908 A. D. It is possible, from the development that seems to have taken place, that the earliest migrants arrived somewhere around 600 and were contemporaneous with the Basket-Maker III people.

CHAPTER THREE

THE PUEBLOS

1

We have seen how during the Basket-Maker period the
Indians of the Southwest developed from a nomadic
group of hunters to primitive agriculturalists and began
to settle down; how at the close of their epoch there was
a new type of people who were to develop into the great
builders of the American desert area. These new people
we commonly call the Pueblo Indians. They were the
greatest potters that developed north of Mexico.
Whether they brought with them the true technique of
making pottery or whether their new blood brought
new inventiveness into the region we do not know.
From the gradual but rapid changes that took place in
the early history of ceramics in this region I suspect that
they did not bring with them the art of pottery making
but stimulated it in the region. The Basket-Makers invented pottery, the Pueblos developed it.

The Pueblo culture is divided into five periods, nu-
merically designated one through five. Of these the first
two should probably be fused into one. The remaining
might best be treated as two, pre-Spanish and post-
Spanish. So we really have three principal periods in the

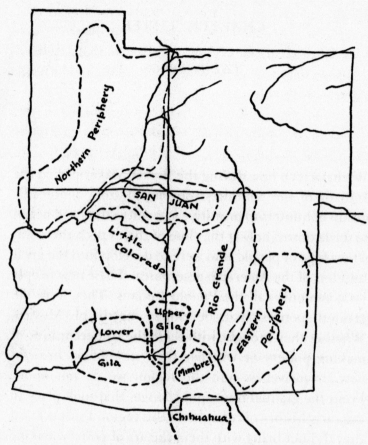

SUBDIVISIONS OF THE PUEBLO CULTURE
(After Kidder)

cultural evolution of this highly civilized group of Indians.* Their early period is characterized by individual or small groups of square houses built of stone and
possibly of adobe. There are left us only the stone struc-

* Since this was written Dr. Frank Roberts has proposed a new nomen-
clature for the stages in the development of the culture which has been

tures. The middle period is represented in Mesa Verde, Sagi Canyon and the Chaco region. After the decline of these three great centers, the population seems to have moved to the east and south and formed the modern era among the Pueblos.

The Pueblo people, as we have pointed out in the preceding pages about the Basket-Makers, were a type physically different from the earlier inhabitants of the region. They were broad-headed and slighter in build than their predecessors and practiced deformation of the head. Among the ruins that have been excavated have been found great numbers of implements and artifacts that tell us of their daily life and culture. They were clever workers in stone and bone, making most of their tools from these two materials. They were better agriculturalists than the Basket-Makers had been. The refuse piles that formed their kitchen middens give us an excellent picture of the variety of their diet. Prac-

---

adopted by the best authorities working in this field. It should be adopted by all and replace the numerical system used in this volume.

ROBERTS'	OTHER DESIGNATIONS
Basket-Maker	Basket-Maker II
	Classic Basket-Maker
Modified Basket-Maker	Basket-Maker III
	Late Basket-Maker
	Post Basket-Maker
Developmental Pueblo	Pueblo I
	Proto-Pueblo
	Pueblo II
	Early Pueblo
Great Pueblo	Pueblo III
	Classic Pueblo
	Golden Age of Pueblo
Regressive Pueblo	Pueblo IV
	Proto-historic Pueblo
Historic Pueblo	Pueblo V
	Post-Spanish Pueblo

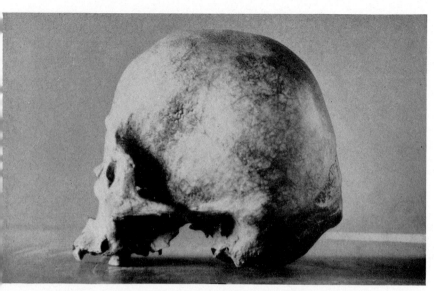

XII CENTURY PUEBLO SKULL, SHOWING DEFORMATION
Canyon de Chelly, Col. Colorado College

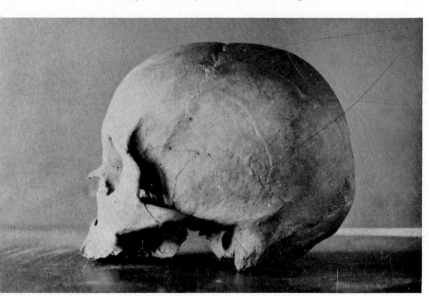

XIX CENTURY PUEBLO SKULL—UNDEFORMED—RIO GRANDE
Coll. A. G. Simms
Photos. by F. M. B.

tically all the mammals and many birds of the region were used for food. At least one bird, the American turkey, was bred but it is doubtful that they used this bird for food. It was apparently reared in order that they might have on hand a constant and plentiful supply of turkey feathers for ceremonial purposes. In their fields they practiced irrigation when necessary, they raised several types of corn, a hard flint corn, a soft starchy corn that could be ground easily to a flour, sweet corn and pop corn. Some of these varieties were yellow, some were red and some were blue-black. In addition to maize, the principal food stuff among the early agriculturalists of America, the Pueblo Indians raised the common string bean, specimens of which have been grown today and proved to be, at least in this one instance, a variety very close to the large Kentucky Wonder bean found in our gardens. Squash of more than one kind is found from the earliest period of the Pueblos and seems to have been developed along with gourds from wild varieties found in the Southwest and in northern Mexico. They used the fruit of many wild plants in addition to these cultivated food stuffs. Acorns, piñon nuts, yucca and practically all of the berries that are found on the mountain sides were in their diet.

As weavers they were very inferior to the people that they displaced. Their basketry was extremely crude and was soon replaced almost entirely by pottery vessels. Their sandals, however, were well made and form one of the characteristics by which they may be differentiated from the earlier people. The Pueblos shaped the front part of the sandal so that it was pointed, not square. They used a different system of tying the sandals to the feet. Their fabrics and cords were made entirely of plant fibers, with cotton and Apocynum string as the basis. Just as the Basket-Maker wove into his cloth fur, the Pueblo wove into his cloth feathers. The appearance of string of vegetable origin, of pointed-toed sandals and primarily of pottery in a Southwest site is a sure indication that it was occupied by these people.

Their small stone unit-houses are abundant in the Canyon country in southwest Colorado, southeast Utah and northeast Arizona. These are made usually of untrimmed stone laid up in irregular courses and tucked into great sheltering caves or crevices in the walls of the canyon. In the Colorado part of their range there are several curious towers, circular or square in shape, that were probably 25 feet or more in height mounted on the tops of the mesas which the canyons dissect. The exact purpose of these towers has not been established. Whether they were used for worship, for defense or as living places we do not know. It is possible, of course, that they served all three purposes. After the discovery of the more highly developed and, of course, much more interesting buildings of the Golden Age, archeologists turned away from the investigation of these minor ruins. Today they offer one of the richest fields for investigation. The paucity of definite information about these

HOVENWEEP CANYON
Ruins of Unit House and Square Tower
Photo. by Laura Gilpin, Colorado Springs, Colo.

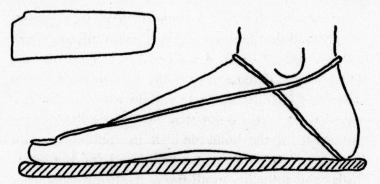

Basket-Maker

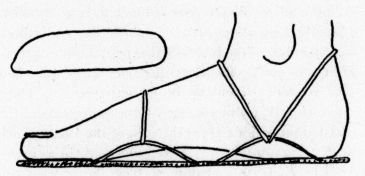

Pueblo

SANDALS

early Pueblos will exist until further excavations are made.

It is possible in traveling from site to site for one to see the gradual development of the Pueblo village. These communities probably developed first as family groups and later for defense against the marauding nomadic tribes that lived to the north and the east. It is interesting to note at this point that among the Pueblos the ownership of the home and all its contents was the women's. The women attended to all the household duties and probably to all the agricultural work. The men were employed in cutting the beams for new roofs, in providing the larder with game, in manufacturing the tools of war and of the hunt and in defending the settlement. As the boys grew older and attained manhood they left their mothers' homes to live together with the other young unmarried men in large, circular, communal dwellings that resembled the semisubterranean homes of the Basket-Maker period. Among these groups of young bachelors there developed the clans that are today found in the modern pueblos. These clubs are still maintained and form the centers of the social and religious life of the men of the village. Each of the clans apparently selected some animal as its adviser or guardian and thus we have the Snake Clan, Coyote Clan, Eagle Clan and others.

As the population increased the communities grew, cities of hundreds of rooms developed in such places as were easily defended. Probably one of the most remark-

BETATAKIN

Photo. by Laura Gilpin, Colorado Springs, Colo.

able and outstanding of these settlements is Cliff Palace at Mesa Verde. Other groups fully as beautiful and well-developed are the ruins of Betatakin and Keetseel in Sagi Canyon to the southwest of Mesa Verde in Arizona. The village of Betatakin is in a far better state of preservation than any in Mesa Verde and will give us a good picture of the settlements of the great period. Here in a huge cave, arching so high above its floor as to dwarf the buildings, is a town of over one hundred rooms. The masonry with which these rooms have been built is not quite so accurately coursed and laid up as at Mesa Verde or in the Chaco. However, it is substantial enough so that not a few rooms are in perfect condition and still retain their roofs. These roofs were made by laying across the tops of the walls wooden beams which were then covered with woven mats of branches and topped by a heavy layer of adobe. Throughout the settlement wattlework walls are evident and from the deep layer of droppings and feathers within these wattle enclosures it is perfectly evident that they were used as turkey coops. The rooms constituting the village are built across the back wall of the cave with frequent courts between them. In front of them, another row was built just behind the retaining wall at the mouth of the cave. In the floor of the cave seven or eight kivas, the name given to the men's clan rooms, are to be found. As yet none of them have been excavated but when they are, they will doubtlessly yield much of interest regarding the clan life in this well-preserved ancient settlement. Along the

wall at one point in one of the courts are great grinding
stones and bins that were used by the women in preparing corn flour. These flat stone metates are abundant
in all the pueblo ruins and were an important part of
household equipment before the advent of the European grist mill. They are still in use today among the
peoples of the pueblos.

Although no burials have been found as yet, they will
doubtless come to light as the great rubbish piles are excavated. In general these were the repositories for the
cast-off frame of man as well as the table leavings, broken
pottery and household rubbish. In the Pueblo burials,
where they are found, the bodies were placed in oval
grave pits dug in the trash piles near the house. Before
burial the bodies were closely flexed and in burial accompanied by pieces of pottery. This makes the task of
the physical anthropologist a good deal easier in tracing
the changes that might have come about in the physical
types of the people during the period of occupancy of
any ruins. The mortuary pottery, where the types are
well-marked, is assignable to a definite cultural period.

Through the studies of Dr. Nelson, Dr. Kidder and
others, we have a very good knowledge of the sequence
of pottery types and their decoration. Although these
cannot be used to establish a true chronological sequence of various pueblos, they are of greatest importance in following the development within any one
pueblo. In the Sagi Canyon region we find three distinct
types of pottery—a corrugated ware in which the origi-

nal coils of clay are marked with incised corrugation for decoration; a black-on-white ware in which a black design is so applied to white pottery that within the band of black the design appears white; and a polychrome ware in which red, black and white are the colors used for decoration. The base color of this polychrome ware is yellow or orange. Apparently the first type was made for large storage jars in which grain was kept throughout the year and for the storage of water. Smaller pots of the same type were used as cooking utensils. The black-on-white ware is very fine grained and hard and extremely well decorated. The common forms of these vessels are water jugs, bowls, ladles and colanders. Small, handled jugs and small seed jars in this type of pottery are much less common. The colanders, which are small jars three to six inches in diameter with a fairly large orifice, are known only from the Sagi Canyon region. Each one has a number of small holes in the bottom evidently fitting it for use as a sifter or strainer. The draftmanship of the decoration is extraordinarily accurate. Apparently the artist laid out a fine grid work of parallel and cross-hatched lines before applying the design of interlocking frets, keys and spirals. These groups of guide lines are the best characteristic by which to recognize the black-on-white ware from this region. The polychrome pottery seems to have been confined to bowls and small, handled jars. These average about ten inches in diameter but larger examples have been found. As in the bowls of black-on-white ware, the design or pattern is found on the inside of the object and is not on the outside except as a line or two often heavy and carelessly drawn circling the neck.

That there was communication and trade between

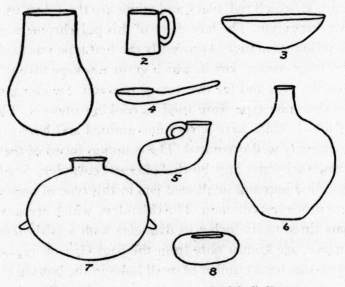

1 Wide mouthed olla	5 "Duck-bodied" pot
2 Mug	6 Narrow mouthed olla
3 Bowl	7 Canteen
4 Ladle	8 Seed bowl

SOME PUEBLO POTTERY FORMS

the great centers at this time, about the close of the 11th century A. D., is evident from the occasional pieces of pottery typical of distant pueblos. It is, of course, natural that such trade should be carried on where a circle seventy-five miles in radius can be drawn that will include three areas of great development. It is surprising, however, to find, as has been found in the Chaco

Canyon, trade materials that must have come from central and southern Mexico. During the excavation of Pueblo Bonito, Dr. Judd found a pot of the type of cloisonné pottery that was manufactured by the people living south of Mexico City. In another room they found the mummified remains of parrots that had been imported from the lowlands occupied by the Maya in northern Central America and southern Mexico.

2

In the history of the Southwest pottery looms large. It is possible to trace, through the developments in ceramics, the development of the culture and even to date ruins in a cultural sequence from the fragments or sherds that are found in them. Unlike most potters in other parts of the world, the Pueblo Indian has never used the potter's wheel for forming her clay vessels. Nevertheless, that has not detracted from the symmetry or beauty of form that she has achieved. The clay used to make the paste from which the bowls and jars were built usually came from banks near the river beds within a few miles of the pueblos. Clays of various colors,—red, gray, white, and yellow,—were used but apparently never mixed in preparing a batch of paste. In order to prevent shrinking, temper was added in most of the pottery. This, too, came from the immediate vicinity of the home of the worker. Sometimes it is volcanic ash, other times disintegrating granite or ground up basalt. The amount of temper used varied with the properties of the clay from practically none to about one-third of the mixture. These raw materials were gathered at infrequent intervals and brought to the pueblo or home of the worker where they were prepared for use. For the clays this preparation consisted in removing all the larger particles by winnowing the dry soil. Similarly the temper was ground and only the finer particles used. The tools employed in shaping the pots are the simplest, pieces of gourd roughly shaped, fragments of broken pots with the edges rounded.

By watching the modern Pueblo potter we have learned how these Indians plied their craft. The first step after kneading enough water and clay together to make a mass with a putty-like consistency that will just crack on pinching is to shape the bottom. This is done by patting out a ball of clay and placing it in a saucer-like implement of baked clay. The walls are built up by taking rolls of the paste and tucking them around the rim of this base, row upon row, until the jar is roughly shaped. Then with a shaper the sides are smoothed down and thinned. These scrapings are saved and used in making other pieces of pottery. When the rough clay has been finally shaped it is set into the sun to dry thoroughly. As a matter of fact, several times during the forming of the pot the modern Pueblo worker sets the incompleted piece aside to dry in order that the lower portion will be firm enough to support the upper part. It takes a good potter twenty minutes to make a small bowl and about five hours to make a large olla. In the case of the latter vessel, the actual working time is probably between one and one-half and two hours and the three hours are taken up with the intermittent drying of the vessel. If during the sun drying the paste cracks badly, it is a sign that insufficient temper has been added to the clay. The piece is then broken up, wet down, more temper added and the paste used again. The final drying in the arid Southwest takes from one to two days. After that a final scraping begins. The portion to be worked upon is moistened and scraped with a sharp implement. In the old days this was probably flint but today it is a case knife or can top. The final polishing is done usually with a piece of sandstone or the soft, spongy part from the inside of a long bone.

The next step is to apply the slip. This slip is made of thin suspensions of colored clays and acts as a sizing to give a uniform background and smooth texture to the piece. All shades of red, yellow and white are the usual slip colors. It is applied with a small mop of cloth or skin. Six or seven coats are applied in rapid succession and wiped smooth. After the slip has dried, it is polished with a smooth, waterworn pebble. This polishing must be done evenly and not too efficiently. Otherwise the slip will have a streaky, polished finish when the bowl is fired. Once the slipping is completed and the surface is dried thoroughly, the design is painted onto the vessel with a brush made from a yucca leaf whittled down to a very fine point such as the old Chinese brushes had. The colors used in painting are black and red and occasionally an orange-red. The two reds are made in the same way as the slips of the same color. The black, however, is quite different. It is in part a vegetable product. To prepare it, in May or June the Indian worker cuts the young shoots of the Rocky Mountain bee-balm or guaco. Then she makes a strong infusion by boiling them in water for a day over a hot fire. The decoction is drained from the fibrous residue and allowed to evaporate in the hot sun to a black mass. Nothing is wasted. The extracted leafy materials and stems are used for food. The extract of guaco is allowed to age for a year or more. The older it is the better paint it makes. To prepare the paint, a pale yellow, limonite clay is put into suspension and mixed with a watery solution of the guaco extract. This dries onto the pot as yellow markings.

The final major step and the most critical one follows. It is the firing. Great care is taken to prepare an even bed of coals and when the potter is satisfied, the oven is built over this bed of coals. The vessels are raised a few inches above the ground to permit firing. Today the framework that holds them is made of iron junk. What was used in primitive times we do not know. After the bowls have been placed upon the grate, a wall-like ring of dung cakes is placed on edge around it with small bits of stone to prevent the cakes from touching the vessels. The fire is now fed fresh fuel and the rest of the oven built of additional cakes of dung. These are placed close together. No attention is paid to the direction in which

BASKET-MAKER III POTTERY, SAN JUAN
Specimens in Taylor Museum, Colorado Springs

PUEBLO I POTTERY, BLACK-ON-WHITE AND CORRUGATED, ARIZONA
Specimens in Taylor Museum, Colorado Springs
Photos. by F. M. B.

the wind blows. The firing takes not much more than half to three-quarters of an hour. After that the oven is broken down and the pots carefully removed to cool. The last step in the case of polished ware is to wipe the piece with a slightly greasy cloth. Other wares are in the finished condition as they are drawn from the heat.

The foregoing briefly outlines the making of pottery in the pueblos today and probably there is very little difference between the techniques of the modern and the ancient potters. Readers who are interested in the details of the art may find it admirably set forth in Dr. Carl E. Guthe's book which is included in the bibliography for this chapter.

3

The various stages through which the archeologists have traced the development of pottery in the Southwest are seven. These have been subdivided and subdivided again but the seven major divisions are sufficient to tell the story. The earliest types of pottery that were made by the pre-Pueblo and Basket-Maker III peoples have survived throughout the history of the art as we see it depicted through excavation. The roughly formed, dark, coiled ware that constitutes the major part of the fragments found in the earliest of the ruins is still made. These crude pots are used for cooking. Their rough exteriors rapidly gather soot and add to their heat conducting ability. As period followed period, the coiled ware improved in that the rolls of clay used became more slender, vessel shapes more symmetrical and varied and, during the classic period, indented designs were applied to the outer surface.

The first of the decorated pottery was made with a white slip decorated in black and is commonly called black-on-white. Interestingly, on this form of pottery in its early stages the decoration, usually geometric, is found only on the inside of the bowls and occasionally on the lip, the outer surface always being free of design. Rarely, in this early type, the slip used was red instead of white and that gave rise to the black-on-red pottery of early sites. When this ware was made with thick walls of a soft and rather spongy paste, it was called biscuit ware. Biscuit ware has survived throughout the development of Southwest ceramics.

The next step in development was the polychrome pottery of prehistoric sites. In this the decoration is in black and white on a red slip. The walls of the vessel are thin and the lip about as thick as the body. Such ware is now being imitated by many of the potters at Zuni, Acoma, Santo Domingo and other pueblos. It is called painted ware to differentiate it from the next development in which the coloring matter was mixed with ground felspar or some other substance that vitrified upon firing. The decoration on polychrome pottery is smooth. The glazed ware, as those pieces with vitrified design are called, may be divided into three principal types. Two of them are prehistoric and the other has been made since the Conquest by the Spaniards. The

PUEBLO II–III, BLACK-ON-WHITE, CHACO CANYON

PUEBLO III, BLACK-ON-WHITE, MESA VERDE

PUEBLO III, KAYENTA BLACK-ON-WHITE JUGS AND MIM-
BRES POLYCHROME BOWL
All above Specimens in Taylor Museum, Colorado Springs
Photos. by F. M. B.

Mesa Verde

Chaco

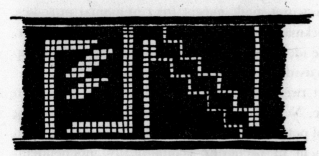

Kayenta

STEP DESIGN ON "BLACK-ON-WHITE" POTTERY FROM SAN JUAN AREA
(After Kidder)

earlier pieces of the glazed ware have a black or deep brown vitrified design on a red, yellow or gray slip. The later of the prehistoric glazed pots are an interesting combination of black glaze and red paint on slips that may be gray, yellow, pink or red. In pottery of this type the black glaze was used to outline the decoration while the pattern itself was filled in with the red paint. The historic glazed ware reverts to the earlier prehistoric type in color combination. However, it seems that the potters had learned from the Spaniards how to mix a superior glaze but did not know how to control it. This has resulted in a pottery easily identified by the running and streaking of the brown or greenish-black glazed patterns on gray, red or yellow slips.

The pottery of modern times, as I have said, is a painted ware. Up to the beginning of the present century it was not made except for ceremonial purposes. The workmanship and decoration are of high caliber. It can be identified by the pink slip or pale orange slip that was used almost uniformly.

About twenty years ago a small group of people in Santa Fe, New Mexico, became interested in reviving the art of pottery making among the Pueblos in order to assist them in becoming economically independent. Since that time tremendous strides have been made in the technique of making painted ware and in reviving many of the ancient motifs in decoration. Mr. Kenneth Chapman of the Laboratory of Anthropology in Santa Fe, through his constant encouragement, has been prob-

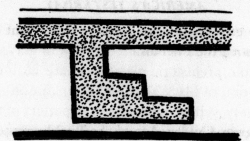

PECOS GLAZE V POLYCHROME: STIPPLE INDICATES
RED

MIMBRES BLACK-ON-WHITE
(Both after Kidder)

ably the greatest moving force in this recent development among the Pueblos.

4

The great Golden Age of the Pueblo people ended abruptly. For years archeologists did not realize how abruptly the great centers like Mesa Verde were deserted nor the reason that the Old People had for giving up such admirably built and easily defended home sites. It was not until Dr. Douglass of the University of Arizona applied to the logs taken from these old buildings his method for dating by tree rings that the story became clear. We have just been going through a period of comparative dryness that has greatly affected our life. Imagine a period of twenty-three years of drouth so great that within that time trees received not enough moisture to enable them to grow as much as they normally would in a single year. It was such a condition, not disease or invasion, that drove the Pueblo people from their safe towns in the canyons of the Four-corners region.

Between 1276 and 1299 A. D. the great drouth of the Southwest occurred. During the first few years of it some new construction was carried on in these ancient cities but soon the land on the mesa tops and in the deeply cut canyons no longer could support a crop of maize sufficient to feed the population. As food became scarce the people slowly scattered we know not where. We have evidence that a few remained at Mesa Verde well on into the drouth. Almost every little gully contains the remains of tiny dams built by these Indians in an effort to store water as this part of the world dried out. But probably before 1290 all the springs vanished and all man's ingenuity had failed to preserve enough of the life-giving fluid to support a single family in the region. Whether they moved north or south, east or west, it is impossible to tell. There are some indications that they may have moved south to be found in Canyon de Chelly. And at the foot of the great cave that houses Casa Blanca, an old ruin from the early 12th century, there seems to have been some attempt to rehabilitate a deserted pueblo. The stream in the canyon, wandering back and forth across its bed, had ripped out some of the walls in the lower houses. These have been repaired with a Mesa Verde-like masonry which differs markedly from that used in the original construction. Occasional sherds are found on the surface at the ruin that show a Mesa Verde type of decoration. The same is true of several other sites that seem to have been abandoned and then reoccupied but no place has been found where the peoples from the drouth stricken region lived for any length of time.

Two solutions to the enigma are possible. Either the people were massacred wholesale by marauding bands of nomads while on their migration or they were ab-

sorbed in small groups by the pueblos to the south and
to the east which were not so sorely affected by the
change in climate. There are some indications that they
may have strayed as far as Scott City on the Arkansas in
Kansas. There have been found the remains of a small
pueblo occupied for a very short time. It seems that
north of Raton Mountain in the Colorado mountains
there was little or no chance for a settled, peaceful people such as these to live. That region was the domain of
the warring, hunting tribes of the plains and the fate of
the Scott City pueblo was probably sealed with a quick,
murderous attack from the Cheyennes or one of their
allies. After the downfall of the Pueblo III people there
seems to have been little difference in the culture other
than the change from building their homes in the protected cliffs of canyons to building large pueblos near
rivers. They had learned their lesson. During the period
just before the Spanish conquest and ever since then,
these people have lived along the Rio Grande, the
Pecos, the Gila and the Mimbres with three notable exceptions: the Zuni and the Hopi towns and the pueblo of
Acoma. These three are all situated in the Mesa country near the New Mexico-Arizona line on the periphery
of the area that had been occupied during the great
pueblo age. During this period just before the advent
of the Spaniards, one marked change is to be noted in
the art of pottery—the application of glazed designs
which have been discussed on preceding pages.

5

In 1528 there was wrecked on the Gulf coast a Spanish expedition under the leadership of Pamfilo de Navarez. Few survived but among them was one Cabeza de Vaca and a negro called Esteban. These two wandered far to the northwest and into what is now called the Southwest. They finally reached the Spanish settlements on the Pacific coast of Mexico. During the journey they had heard of fabulously rich cities lying to the north of their route. Any riches in the New World interested the Spaniards so Mendoza, the Governor of New Spain, sent a Franciscan monk, Fray Marcos de Nizza, with Esteban as interpreter into the newly reported country. They left New Spain in 1539. When they reached the first of the fabled cities that have come to be called the Seven Cities of Cibola, Esteban was several days' journey ahead of Nizza. Just what happened will never be known but Esteban was imprisoned and shortly killed. His fleeing Indian escort brought the news to Nizza. After viewing one of the cities from a long distance, Nizza was so impressed by what he saw that when he at last returned to Mexico his accounts inflamed the minds of the gold-hungry Spaniards. The next year Mendoza placed a large and well-equipped expedition under the command of Vasquez de Coronado. Long, thirsty marches and lack of provisions hardly put the Spaniards into a good frame of mind for

the disappointment that was before them. The mud
cities contained no great treasure and the people were
by no means friendly. These first North American
towns to fall into the possession of the invading Europeans were the Zuni villages in western New Mexico.
There the Spaniards stayed to rest themselves and their
horses and to recuperate from their strenuous journey.
During the period of resting, Coronado received a dep-
utation from the surrounding country even as far as the
Pecos River, half way across the state.

The story of the Pueblos from then on for over one
hundred years is one of mutinous submission to Spanish
rule. In 1680, seventy-five years after the establishment
of the city of Santa Fe, the Indians threw off the Spanish
yoke and for twelve years no foreigner dared to enter
the land. For the first few years there was unanimity
among the Indian tribes. This did not last long. So in
1692 it was possible for de Vargas who had become governor to march northward and by diplomacy and a
strong display of arms receive the submission of all the
pueblos without bloodshed. Unfortunately for him, he
did not spend the winter in the country but went back
to Mexico. The next year when he returned he found
all the Indians turned against him and it was not until
1700 that New Mexico and the Southwest were again
at peace and under Spanish rule.

During the time of the Spanish and later the American control over the Southwest, the native arts and
crafts declined. The chief mediums of barter on the

part of the civilized peoples were cloth and household utensils. Since the metal ware was so much more durable than pottery and stone tools, it is not surprising that the primitive people soon abandoned their own wares and adopted the European implements. Apparently some pottery was made but not much of it and it was not until Dr. Fewkes showed some old Zuni beautifully decorated pottery that he had recovered from prehistoric sites that the ceramic art revived. With this slight start and the more recent encouragement under the leadership of the Santa Fe group that I have already mentioned, pottery making has gained the importance in which it is found today. It has been the one great factor in developing the economic independence of the Pueblo people, just as the weaving of blankets has greatly assisted the seminomadic Navajos.

CHAPTER FOUR

THE VALLEY OF MEXICO

1

MOVING southward from the land that we have just been discussing to the tropical regions, we find many indications of ancient civilization. It was in this area, which we will call Middle America, that the great cities of the Aztecs, the Mayas and other tribes of American Indians were built. The term Middle America is much more applicable to the area from the archeological as well as biological point of view than the designations Mexico and Central America. From the middle of Mexico southward to the Isthmus of Panama, the culture of the primitive people was more or less homogeneous and varied greatly from that in northern Mexico and in the United States. The country may be divided into three geographic zones running from north to south. A rather broad, low, densely tropical coastal region is found on the east; a much narrower and drier coastal region fronts on the Pacific Ocean; and between them are the mountains and the high plateaus where the climate is temperate. It is in this highland plateau that the earliest remains of a somewhat civilized people have been found in America.

The present state of our knowledge of the archeology of Middle America is very spotty. Of some regions we have learned much. Of others we are entirely ignorant.

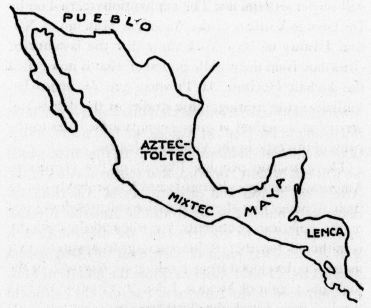

THE MEXICAN CULTURE AREAS

Probably the most extensive exploration of the archaic settlements in the region have been made in the great plateau of Central Mexico. There towns were in existence three or four thousand years ago. A more precise chronological dating of these ruins will be possible only when a more precise dating of the great lava flows found in the region is made. At least two ruins, that are by no means the earliest known, are found beneath the thick cap of the Pedregal lava sheet. These are situated near Copilco and Cuicuilco, just south of Mexico City. To the northeast, but still in the immediate neighborhood, have been found the mounds of debris that were still earlier settlements. The explorations carried on by Dr. George Vaillant of the American Museum of Natural History of New York show that the lava-buried cities date from the middle period of what is now called the Archaic Horizon. At Ticoman and Zacatenco Dr. Vaillant made stratiographic studies of the debris and arrived at a method of giving comparative dates to the ruins of this type in the Valley of Mexico.

These archaic peoples, like all of the peoples of America, were agriculturalists and it is probably due to their strivings that the great maize cultures developed on the American continents. For when all the evidence is gathered together it becomes quite apparent that maize was developed from a wild grass, *teocintli,* in the highland region of Mexico. Like all primitive agriculturalists these people developed to a high degree the art of pottery making. Their pottery, however, differs markedly from that found among the Pueblo people. Among the latter not a great number of shapes were used. Their artistry expanded in the decoration of their pottery. Among the archaic Mexicans the great development took place in the shapes and the decorative design apparently suffered.

Probably the greatest characteristic of these people is the presence in their culture of the manufacture of thousands upon thousands of small clay images or figurines. The major portion of these very clearly represent the female form and are believed to be tokens of fertility to the gods of agriculture. Dr. Vaillant considers the variations among these figurines as primary time-bearers for dating the archaic cities of ancient Mexico. From the artifacts of other types we learn that the people were only fair workers in stone. Their method of flaking and finishing is indicative of a decadent stone-age culture. In general they used flint for the manufacture of their weapons and tools that needed sharp edges. In some regions there seems to have been a tendency toward stone sculpture but this did not develop to a great degree at such an early time. We know very little of their ability as weavers. The wet climate that prevails throughout their domain prevented the preservation of more than one or two small fragments of such materials.

Of the people themselves little is known. Although the excavations have yielded well over a hundred skeletons, no studies as yet have been made of the material and thus no conclusions can be drawn as to their ethnic relationship with their successors or the primitive peoples surrounding them. Like the Pueblos they used their refuse piles and abandoned rooms for burials. That they were imbued with what appears to be a uniform tendency in America to build pyramids and mounds we do know, for each of the sites excavated has been related to some such structure. It seems, however, that they had not yet developed either the idea or the ability to cut stone for their buildings. All the remains

that have been found are made of rounded river stones
set in mud. Because of this it is possible that we will
never know a great deal about their architectural developments. But also because of this we may infer that
they were of a low type.

The pottery that has been recovered is by no means
crude so we may well look forward to the discoveries of
much more primitive people of a sedentary type who,
like the Basket-Makers in the Southwest, invented the
ceramic art in Middle America. There are three recognized divisions of this period in Mexico and, when excavations have been made in the rest of the region, we may
be sure that additional and similar divisions will be
found throughout the area. The early level is characterized by the preponderance of undecorated pottery.
In general it is classified by the color of the slip that was
used into bay, black, white and yellowish wares. It seems
that certain colors of slips were more commonly used
with one form than another. For instance, almost all
the ollas of the period are of the bay ware while the
black and the yellowish wares were used almost exclu-
sively for bowls. Most of the articles produced in the
white ware were shallow dishes supported by three teat-
like legs. Occasionally this white ware was decorated
with a red slip paint. Decoration on the other wares,
when it did occur, was merely incised design.

The little clay figurines of the early period are quite
characteristic. In general they were modeled with long
legs and abbreviated but well-shaped trunk, short, pro-

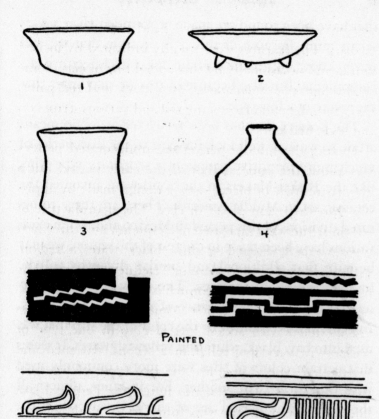

PAINTED

INCISED

ARCHAIC POTTERY
(After Vaillant)

1. Bowl
2. Tripod bowl

3. Jar
4. Olla

jecting arms and an elongated head surmounted by a turban. The features were usually indicated by incised marks and occasionally by tiny added bits of clay. Some of the figures are decorated with black and red paint, the hands, feet and face being red and various stripes on the body black.

During the middle period the undecorated pottery was about the same as that of the early period but a goodly number of pieces show a design made by applying thin strips and pieces of clay. The manufacture of red-on-white ware increased in frequency and three new types were developed—a thin, black ware, a red-on-yellow, and an orange glaze or "lacquered" ware. The figurines of the period are much less artistic. The workmanship is extremely crude. Almost all of the features are modeled with added bits of clay in one type or sculped in very low relief in a second flattened and broadened type. These are the two types of figurines that are found in the remains under the Pedregal lava flow. At Zacatenco they were found in the middle layers of the debris and thus we are able to place in cultural sequence the two buried cities.

The late period is characterized by a decrease in the use of the plain types of pottery that were so abundant in the early period. The chalky white ware of the early period and the fine black ware of the middle period are absent. Several new wares appear. A clear dun-colored slip and a rich brown slip seem to have been developed during this late period. These colors were applied to

EARLY

EARLY

LATE

LATE

MIDDLE

ARCHAIC FIGURINES
(After Vaillant)
(From Photographs)

both the inside and the outside of the pieces while in the earlier periods only the outside and the inside of the neck of the vessel were slipped. At the same time a polychrome ware appears. Upon the basis of pottery the buried ruins of Cuicuilco are related to the late period of Zacatenco, the ruin we are using as a time scale in this chapter. The figurines are worse than those of the middle period, if that is possible. The features are built up with little bits of clay and the sex of the image is very clearly marked. Among the figurines of the late period a departure from all the others is seen in the application of a slip to a very large percentage of those that have been found.

From all the indications it would appear that fully three thousand years ago the peoples of Central Mexico were at about the same cultural level as those of our Southwest at the time of the Spanish Conquest. There is nothing to indicate, however, that the two cultures are related other than the use of maize by both of them. Apparently in both regions the ceramic art developed independently. The fact that its greatest development in the north was a matter of decoration and in the south a matter of form would indicate their non-interdependence even without our knowledge of the complete history of pottery making in the Southwest. We have still to discover in Middle America the cultural horizon equivalent to the Basket-Makers. Our chance for doing so appears at present to be very slim. In the pre-pottery stage the utensils must have been made of basketry or weaving. The climatic conditions of Middle America militate against such fragile remains existing for the long period of time. It is only in extremely arid regions such as our Southwest that conditions prevail fostering the preservation of such handicraft. There are, however, a few areas on the western coast of Mexico to which the archeologist may turn in search for the equivalent of the Basket-Maker horizon. As yet nothing has been found.

2

The term time-bearer has been borrowed by the archeologists from the geologists to denote artifacts or characteristics that date a phase in the development of a culture. Until a large number of sites have been examined no really adequate series of time-bearers can be set up. However, it is possible in a single excavation to establish a sequence that will naturally aid in arriving at conclusions regarding a restricted area. Although they have not been so labeled a number of time-bearers have been indicated in the foregoing chapters. The earliest of these are the geological time-bearers of glacial sands and gravels. Each one of the successive glaciations had a slightly different range and by carefully studying the gravel deposits and their superimposition it is possible to arrive at a logical sequence of deposits that may be applied throughout the area affected by all the glaciers. So, for the paleo-anthropologists who are studying the remains of pre-man and especially the remains of man in the glacial period, these gravels are time-bearers. In connection with the actual gravels themselves are the accumulations of remains of extinct animals. For the period of time that the world has been inhabited by man has been one during which great changes have taken place in the fauna of the various continents. Thus the presence of human bones or artifacts in undisturbed gravels that also contain the remains of the giant ground-sloth date the presence of man as contemporaneous with those sloths. The remains of man have been found associated with ground-sloths in Nevada and in the Mississippi Valley. The geological dating of the deposits in Nevada is extremely difficult because of the lack of glaciation in that area, while the beds in the Mississippi Valley that contain the deposits just mentioned can be associated with one of the early periods of glaciation. Since it is probable that the ground-sloth became extinct throughout the United States at relatively the same time, we can place some confidence in the opinion that the finds at Gypsum Cave, Nevada represent those of a man that inhabited the United States during the early glacial times.

Another type of time-bearer is associated not with actual time but with cultural development. As an example of this may be given the method in preparing tools from flint. From the deposits in France we have seen that there was a gradual evolution of technique from percussion shaping to pressure shaping. Students of flint work use this and the variety of shapes and implements formed as time-bearers of culture. However, there is a vast difference in the interpretation that may be implied from geological time-bearers and cultural time-bearers. The first type gives us positions in actual time while the second type indicates the extent to which a culture has developed. Thus at the same time the two extremes of time-bearers of the cultural variety may exist without conflict, merely indicating that the two peoples had not reached the same levels of development.

In the Southwest the great time-bearers are basketry and pottery. The presence of considerable basketry and the absence of pottery at a site indicate that the site is earlier than one in which pottery predominates. Among the pottery producing peoples it has been possible to work out a sequence of development in the ceramic art that seems to apply the world over for placing the cultural development of people. The earliest stage is one characterized by extremely crude pottery of the simplest utilitarian shapes and completely lacking in decoration. The next step seems to have been the evolution of a more finished product and its decoration with incised designs. The third division is that of the decoration of pottery by means of slips and paints. In general the earliest decorated pottery is very simply adorned with geometric designs contrasting in color with the slip. A higher type is represented by polychrome decorations and realistic designs drawn from nature. Further development is indicated by the stylization of the design and then its decadence. The next great move in ceramics seems to be a multiplication of shapes accompanied by a decoration that is so decadent as to appear extremely primitive. Gradually this multiplicity of shapes settles down to a conventional group, part of which is designated serviceware and is used in the ordinary household routine, another part of which is associated with the religious ceremonies of the people. Frequently the latter group represents a more fixed type and shows rich variation over long periods of time. During the development of a culture manufacturing a great variety of pottery shapes, the designs used to decorate the pottery go through a cycle similar to that through which they passed when associated with simple forms. An off-shoot of the multishaped pottery is the effigy pot which is formed as a piece of clay modeling representing either man or some object. Such pottery is best exemplified in the Chimu culture of Peru and will be discussed at length later on. The highest development which pottery gains is the stylized design on a stylized form in a culture represented by many forms. Thus the ceramic art lends itself admirably to use as a cultural time-bearer and through it primarily we are led to date the so-called Archaic culture of Mexico as a higher one than the Pueblo culture of the southwestern states, although the latter reached its zenith probably three thousand years later.

Among the time-bearers for the Archaic culture of Mexico ceramics supply two items that are probably better fitted to trace the development than the pots themselves. These two are the clay figurines and clay earplugs. I have already mentioned the development that took place in the manufacture of the figurines. The earplugs are just as indicative of cultural relationships

EARLY   MIDDLE

LATE

ARCHAIC EARPLUGS
(From Photos by Vaillant)

as the figurines and, since they are simple objects, a little easier to classify. Apparently the earliest types of earplugs were simple discs cut from pot sherds. The first development in the manufacture of earplugs was to imitate these discs and so the earliest earplugs found lack decoration of any kind. Just as in pottery, the earliest modification is the addition of an incised design. Gradually these designs became more and more complex and the plugs more finished products. The ultimate form and the natural one is a pierced design in which the decoration is cut out of the plug.

Architecture is also an extremely good cultural time-bearer. Thus far we have taken man from a period in which he led a nomadic life and had no true architecture to a period of permanent buildings. The earliest development of habitations was probably the enlargement of semisubterranean cists similar to those used for the storage of crops and roofed with logs and sod or thatch of some variety. Man's next endeavors in building were almost entirely on the surface of the ground but still circular or semicircular in shape. The third stage may be represented by rectangular buildings of one or two rooms. This naturally led to the construction of the huge communal buildings upon a rectangular base.

The fact that man began to live in large and protected communities seems to have brought about unemployment for the men. In order to occupy their time the warriors and defenders of settlements organized the various cults that developed into clans, each with its group of ceremonies. In other words, a formal religion was developed to occupy the time of the men when they were not out hunting or waging war. It is interesting that the next step in the architectural development of primitive peoples, at least as it appears in America, was the decadence of the home and the development of religious edifices. Among most of the Middle American people that we will discuss in the next few chapters, it is only these religious buildings that have remained. The dwellings were so insubstantial that hardly a trace of them is left. Among the Mexican aborigines of high development these ruined temples carry the best of all time-bearers, architectural decoration and actual calendar dates. Through a study of both of these together it is possible to trace the development from simple buildings to those more complex, from simple geometric, decorative sculpture through a realistic style to a highly stylized form and then through the usual sequence of decadence.

Throughout the rest of this book time-bearers for individual cultures will be continually cropping out but it must be borne in mind that such cultural time-bearers indicate cultural sequence, not chronological sequences in the narrow sense of year dates.

3

Too little is known at this time to explain the connection between the Archaic culture in Mexico and the much more advanced civilizations to which we will now turn. There is a hiatus of probably two thousand years and possibly much longer of which we know nothing. There are indications that show that the Toltec people derived much of their civilization from the Archaic.

Yet we cannot ascribe to them a very early date. The Aztecs, in turn, absorbed the Toltecs almost completely. There seems to have been some connection between the Toltecs and the Mayas during the last centuries of the Maya civilization and there seems to have been some connection between the Zapotec and allied cultures and the Maya. So it will be impossible to treat the four great centers of antiquity in Mexico without reference to each other and this may cause at some points slight confusion.

Since the Toltecs seem to have derived many of their cultural characteristics from the Ancient Ones, we will look into this culture first.

When the Spaniards arrived in Mexico and some of them began gathering the histories and customs of the people, they learned of a race that had occupied previously the great temperate tableland. These predecessors the Aztecs called Toltecs. The derivation of that name is today a bit hazy. There seem to be two adequate etymologies. It may mean "Builder-People" or "People of Tula." I prefer the first derivation since the Toltecs were the first of the great builders in Middle Mexico and their influence can be seen throughout almost all of Middle America. Of the people themselves we have little knowledge. Some of the Aztec historians referred to them as giants, probably because of the stupendous archeological monuments they left behind them. What skeletal remains have been found have not as yet been studied but there is nothing to indicate that they were any larger people than is normal today throughout the region. A dozen or so of their old cities have been excavated and studied by archeologists from Germany, England, the United States and Mexico. They were the first people in the central part of Mexico to have developed the pyramid complex on a grand scale. One of these structures covers an area twice that of the largest Egyptian pyramid, Cheops at Giza.

The stone tools associated with the ruins are good but by no means outstandingly well formed or worked. As is usual with the higher primitive civilizations, the pottery affords us the most interesting study. Pots, jugs, figurines and earplugs or their fragments are abundant in the debris. In addition to these there occur sparingly whistles, flageolets and extremely complex incense burners. It is among the figurines that we find the most reliable indicators of the Toltec people. The earliest, like those of the preceding Archaic people, are well modeled but they differ in one important character— they are clothed. Among the later figurines a complete departure in manufacture is observed—that of molding. By this process baked molds of clay were made and the soft paste of the figurine pressed into them, the mold separated, and the model fired and painted. In general the face and dress is painted red and the complicated headgear yellow. Another still later step in the development of these interesting bits of pottery is the manufacture of tiny images in which the head and torso were modeled in one piece and the arms and legs separately.

These jointed figurines were fastened together by means of perforations through the shoulders and hips. The medium used for making the joint was probably sisal. A third innovation was the manufacture of products that had the head alone modeled of clay, the body and appendages made of some less durable substance that, during the ages through which the specimens have been buried, has disappeared. Toward the close of the Toltec period many of the figurines became highly stylized and represent specific gods. One that appears quite frequently is that of Xipe, the flayed god of the Aztecs. Other agricultural deities and goddesses are found also so we may believe that the figurines still played an important part in the agricultural religion of these people. A type of clay miniature that was extremely rare in the lower horizon, the Archaic, is one figuring an animal. Among the Toltecs a great many such objects have been found representing the serpent head, the ocelotl and the owl.

The pottery differs rather markedly in the treatment of the decoration. Although the usual painted type is quite common, there is an abundance of pottery in which the decoration does not depend upon color. These new methods may be grouped roughly into five classes. The first is a very carefully incised ware upon which complicated and highly decorative designs have been incised accurately before baking. These designs may be purely abstract and geometric or may represent such complex figures as completely equipped warriors.

The design of the second type is usually less complex and is in the form of added ribbons or balls of clay that may or may not be modeled separately, so placed as to give a distinctive pattern. For another type of decoration the Toltecs made stamps of clay and impressed these forms upon the drying paste of the pot before it was fired. An interesting method of decoration gives us a fourth type. For this, decorative motifs were modeled in clay or more frequently molded and applied to the outside of the piece and baked into place. The decoration of such molded ware is often very beautiful and intricate. The last type of pottery decoration that seems to be characteristic of the Toltecs is a sort of batik technique applied to pottery in which the design was painted on the object in a resinous or waxy substance, then the entire surface slipped with a color. But of all the ceramics of this period the most complex and to me the most interesting are the incense burners. The base of these implements is a shallow dish on a staunch pedestal and carries little decoration. The cover is usually three to four times as high as the burner proper and is highly decorated with molded designs called *adornos* applied to it. Frequently some god head is the major figure of the upper portion and is surrounded by the various symbols used to denote that deity. It is impossible to describe adequately the bizarre beauty of these utensils.

Apparently the Toltecs contributed to the Mexican civilization the game *tlachtli,* a very early forerunner of basket ball, that possibly spread from the Maya empire. The game will be discussed in the chapter dealing with that group of people. The Toltecs also are credited with the invention of pulque, a fermented drink made from the Agave and to this day an important Mexican product.

These people lived toward the close of the first millenium of the Christian era. They carried on extensive intercourse with the civilizations to the south of them, influencing those regions and, in turn, receiving much from their neighbors. We have particularly detailed information concerning the relationship of the Toltecs and the Mayas. Most of this will be discussed in a later chapter. It is enough to say at this time that the Toltec warriors hired out as mercenaries to the League of Mayapan in Yucatan. At about that time, somewhere in the 12th century, A. D., there arose a great figure in Middle American history, Quetzalcoatl, who later became deified throughout the region. He is credited with carrying the Maya calendar back to the Valley of Mexico and establishing it there around 1200 A. D. According to Dr. Spinden the initial date, 1 *Tecpatl,* corresponds with August 6, 1168 in our calendar. It is quite probable that the date commemorates the birth of Quetzalcoatl.

Some of the better known Toltec ruins are these. Tula, "The Place of the Reeds," which is supposed to be the site from which these people sprang, was still occupied at the time of the Spanish Conquest. From the

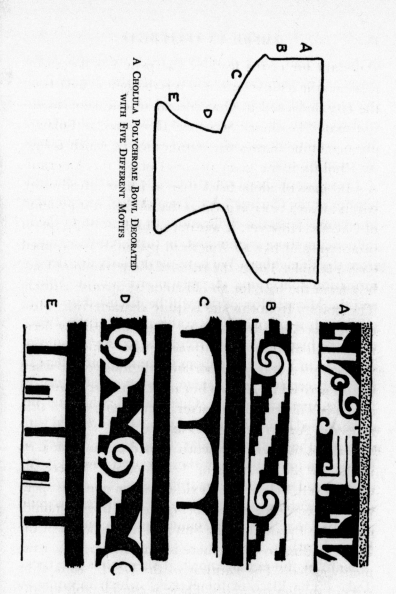

A Cholula Polychrome Bowl Decorated with Five Different Motifs

abundant use of the feathered serpent as a decorative motif on the temple buildings it is thought to have been the city dedicated to Quetzalcoatl whose name means just that—"Feathered Serpent." Here, too, at Tula are gigantic stone figures the significance of which is lost. At Cholula is the giant pyramid of all the Americas. A solid mass of adobe brick that, as I have already said, covers an area twice as great as that of the great pyramid of Cheops. However, it was not so high as its Egyptian prototype and like all American pyramids was capped with a temple. Today the ruins of the pyramid of Cholula form the base for an old colonial Spanish church. The pottery from this site is quite characteristic. Most of the pieces are flat dishes or plates beautifully decorated with all-over polychrome design. This city, too, was occupied and an important religious center when Cortez arrived in Mexico but most of the accumulated debris is Toltecan in character, there being only a thin veneer of Aztec trash on the surface.

Perhaps the most frequently visited of the Toltec remains are the pyramids of Teotihuacan, "Where the Gods Dwell." Here the Mexican government has spent years in excavating and restoring the two huge pyramids called the Pyramid of the Sun and the Pyramid of the Moon leading to which there is a broad roadway, commonly called "The Pathway of the Dead," flanked by rows of smaller pyramids. There is considerable affinity in the sculpture found at Teotihuacan with that found in the Maya cities and so we are led to believe that the

PYRAMID OF THE SUN, TEOTIHUACAN

(Courtesy, Department of Publicity, the Mexican Government)

great structures at least were built after the return of the Toltec mercenaries from Yucatan. Just as this city shows Maya influence, so Xochicalco on the southwestern border of the Toltec area shows the influence of the Zapotec people who built the great city of Monte Alban.

The great majority of the ancient cities of the Mexican highlands are in such ruinous state that they are difficult to study from an architectural standpoint. They were situated in the region that the Spaniards populated most densely and provided a convenient supply of ready cut stones for the haciendas, churches and roads that the invaders built. In the south and southeast the climate was less fit for Europeans and the soil much less fertile or else covered with dense, swampy jungle. It is in that region that we find today the tumbled mounds of the Maya cities. Through the careful exploration and excavation of these, archeologists have pieced together a great fund of knowledge concerning the Maya civilization. Let us now turn to it.

CHAPTER FIVE

LIFE AMONG THE MAYA PEOPLE

1

WITH all the grandeur that remains of the temples and religious edifices throughout the Maya country, it is surprising that we know little or nothing of the homes of these interesting people. However, between the wall paintings that remain in a few of the ruins and the type of home that is built today there is such a marked similarity that one is led to believe that the architecture of the home has not changed with the Spanish Conquest. The predominating shape of the Maya Indian's house today is oblong with semicircular ends. The walls are made of wattle plastered with mud. The roof is palm thatch supported by two poles across which is laid the roof tree, the folded palm leaves being woven into a loose frame work of light poles. The floor is dirt and the furnishings simple wooden stools and low tables. These low objects are quite similar to those seen in the drawings made hundreds of years ago. The fireplace and stove is a crude thing made of three stones. It is usually outside the house. Today cheap tinware has replaced the stone and pottery cooking utensils but the calabash is still used for water.

From the various accounts left us by the invading
Spaniards and from the great mass of sculptured figures,
we can draw a very accurate picture of the clothing
worn in the heyday of these people. The men wore waist
girdles made of cotton cloth caught up between the
legs. The cloth was embroidered with marginal designs

A MAYA HOUSE AND WOMAN GRINDING MAIZE

in colored thread or feathers. Around their shoulders
they wore light cotton mantles, the margins, too, embroidered. This was the sole dress of the general population. The nobility and militia wore further articles of
clothing. The most highly prized was a headdress of
feathers taken from the Quetzal bird, one of the sacred
animals of the people. Necklaces and gorgets of jade,
turquoise, shell and later on gold were worn by all people of importance. They, too, wore belts or sashes about
their waists. When made of leather, these belts were
studded with jade and turquoise. Armlets and leglets
decorated with feathers, jewels and later metals added
to the ornamentation. Practically everyone wore ear-

plugs of one form or another, some of them so large that the lobes of the ears almost touched the shoulders. A curious, crooked noseplug seems to have been worn by the elite and the warriors. The clothing of the priesthood was similar to that of the laymen but included a flowing gown that reached from the neck to the ankles. The women wore but a single garment, a fine cotton skirt reaching from just above the ankles to under the breasts which were usually tattooed and exposed. The hem of this garment was decorated with embroidery.

These people had a curious idea of beauty. To satisfy it the heads of infants were lashed between two boards so that they could grow only upward. This resulted in the curious conical heads seen so frequently in the sculptured representations of men. Another mark of beauty was crossed eyes. In order to bring about such a high desired condition, little beads were suspended from the forelock of infants so that they dangled over the bridge of the nose. Thereby a squint and a crossing of the eyes was caused. Numerous skulls have been found in which the teeth have been filed or inlaid with semiprecious stones and iron pyrites. Tattooing was resorted to for further personal adornment by both sexes.

The warrior in battle array wore a heavy quilted armor of cotton some three inches thick protecting him from the neck to below the knees. His armament consisted of bows and arrows, spear throwers, long swords and shields. The bow and arrow was probably intro-

duced into the Maya area at the time of the Toltec
mercenaries. There is even some evidence that the
earliest of the Maya people did
not use the spear thrower and
that it, too, migrated in from
the Valley of Mexico. The native weapons of offense seem to
have been the sling shot and the
blow pipe, the weapon of defense a long sword made of sapote wood and edged with numerous flint blades as sharp as
razors. The shields were made
of the hides of deer and jaguar
stretched on wooden frames.
Another type was a tightly
woven plaque of reeds. It is apparent from some of the acces-
sories that much was done to
instill fear in the enemy. Others
may have been fetiches and personal or group insignia. Drums
and conches were used to in-

A MAYA WARRIOR EQUIPPED
WITH THROWING STICK, DARTS,
ARM SHIELD, PADDED SLEEVE,
BACK AND KNEE SHIELDS
(In the Manner of the Wall
Paintings)

crease the din of human voices. The warriors went to
battle with hideously painted faces.

From the legends that have come down to us we know
that when war was declared the organization of warfare
was highly ceremonial. Before the first battle was fought
the two armies, bearing with them the image of their

war god, met and exchanged compliments and then set about in what might almost be called a ceremonial battle. However, after this first encounter, as in modern war, everything was fair and ambush and surprises played a great part in settling the fate of an army. It was one of the objects of Maya warfare to capture rather than kill an opponent. Thus was a city supplied with slaves and victims for sacrifices. For the latter rite only those captives of high rank were kept and it was an honor to be so dealt with. Frequently, at least under the Toltec regime in Yucatan, the flesh of the victim was distributed among the multitude and eaten not as food but in order to acquire the noble characteristics and bravery of the sacrificed man.

There is no evidence that the Mayas had standing armies as seems to have been the case in the Valley of Mexico. They had instead a permanent militia whose members during peace time were occupied in the routine of civil life and called from that only in time of war. There were, however, two full time war leaders in each city; one office lasted the life time of the incumbent, the other was an elective office held for three years. The incumbent of the latter was called the Nacom. This position had attached to it considerable form. It was he who arranged the annual feast for the warriors during the month of *Pax*. Throughout the time a man occupied the position he was required to refrain from intercourse with women and to live upon an ordained diet. He must not eat meat other than that of fish and the great iguana lizard and, while he might indulge to a slight extent in alcoholic beverages, under no condition was he allowed to become drunk. Since he was frequently a man of nobility this must have worked some hardship upon him for one of the chief occupations of the noblemen seems to have been feasting and drinking. The women, too, had their feasts but not with the men. There seems to have been no occasion upon which the sexes held banquet together. The men's feasts were far more frequent and it was the duty of the wife to wait outside and take her drunken lord home and put him to bed.

The food of the people, although it lacked much that is common on our tables today, was by no means uninteresting and monotonous. The mainstay, as with most of the American Indians, was maize. This was prepared in many ways, most commonly as tortillas and tamales. The tortilla took the place of bread. It was made by boiling the dried corn, then soaking it in lime water. The hard outer shell was slipped off and the mealy inner portion ground to a fine flour paste on a smooth metate. This paste was patted out into paper-thin wafers and baked on a hot griddle. Occasionally the tortilla was slit and stuffed with mixtures of meat, beans and tomato. The tamales, like those of today, were cornmeal to which was added finely chopped meats or beans or calabash seed and plenty of chili pepper. The mass was then wrapped in corn husks and baked or boiled. Maize, too, was a source of drink—either a gruel or a beer formed from the fermented gruel. Other vegetables that were grown in the milpas were sweet potatoes, squash, beans, tomatoes and sweet mandioc. The diet included such fruits as today grow in the region with the exception of bananas and the citrus fruits. They had plums, avocado pears, papaya, sapote and bread fruit. The cacao from which we today get our chocolate and cocoa was an important part of their diet and economy for it served both as food and money. So much of this product was used in the Maya area that part of their supply had to be imported from the neighboring Mexican states. For meat they relied upon the hunt and their table was supplied with wild boar, coati and venison. Ducks and turkeys were also used and it is quite probable that the turkeys were bred. The sea supplied fish and every rock wall iguana, a large lizard whose tail when baked is a real delicacy. The hunters used on the larger game the bow and arrow but on the iguana and birds a blow gun equipped with clay pellets, not darts, was used. Very important to those of the hunting fraternity was a breed of dogs resembling small greyhounds that were used extensively on the chase. It is also apparent that another breed of dog, much smaller and hairless, was bred for food. Sugar as such was unknown but honey formed an adequate substitute for it and many people were employed in apiculture. In the tropics there is a group of honey bees that are stingless and these are the ones the Mayas employed. In addition to use as sweetening, honey was the source of a very potent wine that figured in every feast and contributed to the gaiety.

The farm land was cultivated by means of a system that today is called milpa. This consisted in the burning off of the jungle and the planting of the seeds in the thin layer of soil topping the fundamental limestone of the peninsula. Agriculture apparently was a communal enterprise and conducted on a very low scale. Once the seeds were planted they were left to do the best they could in competition with the rank brush that grew up with them. This probably accounts for the periodic abandonment of many of the great cities. It was a case of the soil being exhausted and the necessity of finding new and fertile ground for their fields.

2

A remarkable characteristic of all the higher pre-Columbian civilizations in Mexico is their calendars. These are all similar in construction and probably derivatives of the Maya calendar. They are by far the most accurate group of calendars that are known to have existed at the time of the advent of Europeans in the New World and, in fact, are almost identical with the present Gregorian calendar that was not adopted in our country until after 1700 A. D.* The present length of the year is 365.2422 days. The Maya estimate of the year was 0.0002 of a day short of the present year length while our present calendar is 0.0005 of a day longer than

* The Gregorian Calendar was first proposed in 1582.

the true year. It is amazing that a people without the aid of astronomical instruments could develop so accurate an estimate of the length of a year.

The Mayas had two methods for keeping track of time. One system is called the Long Count and the other the Short Count. The Long Count is essentially a count of the number of days that have passed since the institution of their calendar system. That does not necessarily mean that the zero day was actually experienced by the Mayas but that they established such a day in the distant past. A Maya date in this system is usually designated by five numbers, the first of which designates the largest time division and the last of which is a day count. There were twenty days in the Maya month and eighteen of these months constituting a 360-day period were called a *tun*. Twenty *tuns* constituted one *katun* and twenty

PORTION OF THE LINTEL FROM THE TEMPLE OF THE INITIAL INSCRIPTION CHICHEN ITZA SHOWING THE INITIAL DATE 10.2.9–1–9 1 MULUC 7 ZAC

katuns one *bactun*. A little simple arithmetic will demonstrate that one *bactun* contained four hundred *tuns* of 360 days each. This amounts to 394.26 years. The fol-

lowing table shows the methods of writing Maya dates
and the equivalents in our years.

0.0.0–0–1 = 1 kin = 1 day = 0.00274 year
0.0.0–1–0 = 1 uinal = 20 days = 0.0548 year
0.0.1–0–0 = 1 tun = 360 days = 0.9684 year
0.1.0–0–0 = 1 katun = 7200 days = 19.713 years
1.0.0–0–0 = 1 bactun = 144,000 days = 394.260 years

The Short Count is quite differently constituted. It
consists of numbers and names for each day throughout
a cycle of 52 years during which no two days have the
same numbers and names. It in turn is composed of two
counts. One is a short period called the *tzolkin,* of
260 days, through which there is an ever-repeating sequence of thirteen numbers superimposed upon an
ever-repeating sequence of twenty names. We do not
know exactly how this 260-day period originated. There
is no relation at all between it and any natural occurrence. There is, however, a correspondence that may be
accidental, yet at the same time is of exceeding interest.
Two *tzolkins,* 520 days, is approximately the time that
elapses between three eclipses.

Members of the Carnegie Institution working in the
highlands of Guatemala have recently discovered this
religious calendar still in use in some of the most remote
Indian villages. It is remarkable to note that the dates
used vary by only one or two days from those projected
forward from the time of the Spanish Conquest by modern students of the Maya calendar.

The longer period has been called the *haab* but there seems to be no real evidence that this was the Maya name for it. It corresponds most closely with our year and was divided into nineteen months. The first eighteen of these consist of twenty days each, numbered from zero to nineteen and the last is a short month of five days, numbered from zero to four. This use of zero in the mathematics of the Maya people is quite different from that in our system of counting. The Mayas did not consider a day to have a number until it had passed and then in counting it they stated the number of days that had elapsed fully. Thus the first day of any month was considered the zero day since no full day had elapsed since the month began. It may be of interest here to note that our concept of zero came to us through the Arabs from the Hindus who seem to have originated it at some time around 600 A. D. The repeated occurrence of twenty in Maya mathematics is another marked difference between our system of notation and theirs. We use a system based on ten; that is, after we have passed through ten units we go on to numbers in the next order and ten tens make the first number of the third order, 100, and so on. The Maya numerical notations are based on a vigesimal system. In it twenty units in succession must occur in any place * to move the number into the next higher order.

In writing their numbers the Mayas usually arranged

---

* An exception to this is the use of only eighteen groups of twenty units to constitute the third order.

them in a vertical row with the highest position at the top. In the simplest form they used glyphs or symbols to indicate the order or position and a combination of dots and bars to indicate the number in that order. Each dot was equivalent to one and each bar to five.

With these two calendars, the *tzolkin* and the *haab,* starting at the same point it is easy to see that the shorter one would repeat more frequently than the longer one; and, since a day had a number and a name from each of the calendars, a great many more combinations are possible than in our system of a number and month name. As I have already stated, there was no repetition during a period of 52 years. When this system was started we do not know. All calendars have some good reason for starting. The Christian calendar which we use is supposed to date from the birth of Christ. The calendars of many other people date from the birth of outstanding men. Some calendars are supposed to date from the beginning of the world and it is possible that the Mayas had a similar idea for there is known one Maya date that stretches back about five million years into antiquity.

The conversion of Maya dates in their strange form to our more familiar designation is not too difficult. The difficulty lies in tying one Maya date to a specific Christian date. As yet no unequivocal pair of such dates is known. The various authorities who have worked upon the problem have arrived at vastly different conclusions. The widest spread is between the correlations of Joyce

and Förstemann. According to the former, the Maya
date 9.0.0–0–0 is equivalent to the year 95 B. C., while
the latter sets it at 1134 A. D. Of the dozen or so correlations that have been suggested two stand out as being
most plausible. Dr. Sylvanus Morley, using the Chronicles left to us by Mayas at the time of the Spanish Conquest, arrives at the equation 9.0.0–0–0 equals 176 A. D.
Goodman, supported by Dr. John Teeple, sets it at 435
A. D. They base their conclusions upon an exhaustive
study of astronomy. I personally suspect they are both
correct in a measure, since both seem to be equally supported, and that Morley's figures are for the New Empire. In Appendix II an interested reader will find most
of the important Maya dates that have been transcribed
converted into the Christian chronology according to
both of these systems.

And now a word about calculating dates. The Maya
date inscribed upon Temple No. 11 at Copan is a good
one to use since it contains figures in all five places—
9.16.12–5–17. According to Dr. Morley's tables the
katun 9.16.0–0–0 corresponds with 492.193 A. D., when
the days of the year are expressed decimally. The re-
mainder of the Maya date accounts for the elapse of
twelve *tuns,* five *uinals* and seventeen *kin* since that A. D.
date. From the table of equivalents on a preceding page
we see that the *tun* is equivalent to 0.986 year. Therefore twelve of them will be 11.792 years. The five *uinals*
of twenty days each and the seventeen *kin* give us an

additional period of 117 days which is equivalent to
0.321 year. Adding these up we have:

$$9.16.0 -0-0 = 492.193$$
$$12-0-0 = 11.792$$
$$0-5-17 = 0.321$$
$$\overline{9.16.12-5-17 = 504.206 \text{ A. D.}}$$

This is according to Morley's method.

The Goodman-Teeple system places all dates 259.115
years later so by adding this figure to the Morley date
we get their correlation which is 763.321 A. D. By changing the decimal part into days and then into months and
days we arrive at the conclusion that Temple No. 11 at
Copan was dedicated on March 15, 504 (N. S.) * according to Morley and on April 27, 763 (N. S.) * if the
Goodman-Teeple system is correct.

It is probably difficult from the foregoing to see why
the claim is made that the Maya calendar is more accurate than our former Julian calendar when there is
no evidence given here for a more accurate length of a
year than 365 days. That conclusion has been drawn
from a study of what is called the Supplementary Dates.
Almost every important date in the Old Empire is accompanied by a series of glyphs and numbers that tell
the student accurately just how many days have elapsed
since the new moon and since the transit of Venus. It

---

* These dates, although earlier than 1582, are given as though they were
in our present Gregorian or New Style calendar, not the Julian or Old
Style calendar which was current at the times they signify.

is also possible that further undeciphered dates will show that the Maya astronomer priests kept track of such prominent heavenly bodies as Mars in addition to the Sun, the Moon and the planet Venus. We have just begun to appreciate the accuracy of the Maya astronomers.

3

One of the curious points regarding the Maya people is that there is no evidence in the area occupied by them of a culture leading up to theirs. This has set the ethnologists and archeologists searching Mexico and Central America for related peoples whose culture is continuous back to archaic times. The search has been carried on along the coast of the Gulf of Mexico in the neighborhood of Vera Cruz where two groups of Indians, the Huasteca and the Totonaca, are found whose languages belong to the Mayance stock. Another bit of evidence that points to the southward migration of the Maya people is a small jadeite statue that was found near San Andres de Tuxtla. This little figurine is a curious squat image of a man with a duck face. On the front of it is inscribed a Maya date in its simplest form. There is considerable question on the part of the authorities who have examined it whether it represents trade ware that had been brought in or whether it was found near its site of manufacture. There seems to be more weight in favor of the latter opinion. The date upon it expressed in the Maya way is 8.8.2–4–17. According to the correlation with the Christian chronology that I am using this date places its manufacture around 162 A. D. According to Morley's method it would be dated around 97 B. C. This Maya date, 8.6.2–4–17, is the earliest known in all the hundreds that have been deciphered.

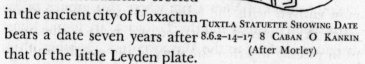

About 140 years later a little tablet was made that had been found in the heart of what we term the Old Empire region of the Mayas. The earliest of the stone monuments erected in the ancient city of Uaxactun bears a date seven years after that of the little Leyden plate.

TUXTLA STATUETTE SHOWING DATE 8.6.2–14–17 8 CABAN O KANKIN
(After Morley)

From that time on stone monuments that have been dated appear throughout the southern part of Mexico and on the peninsula of Yucatan. So it seems that about the dawn of the Christian era saw the settlement of the Mayas in the region that they have occupied for almost two thousand years. At the time of their first settlement they were accomplished architects and astronomers. How long it took them to develop their art and architecture we do not know. It may have been a relatively short period of time. What leads me to believe this is that they apparently had not been building long enough to have developed a true arch. All their buildings have high arched ceilings constructed on the cantilever. In such an architecture the stones forming the roof do not support themselves as do those of the real arch but must be counterbalanced and supported by the stones below. This prevented the builders from roofing a large area. Thus we find among the Maya ruins no room greater than eighteen feet wide and most of them very much narrower. To support the tremendous weight of this type of roof it was necessary to build massive walls. These were pierced by windows only occasionally, all the light and ventilation coming from the doorways.

The buildings that are left for us to study, either as crumbled walls or mounds of debris, were connected almost entirely with the religion. As such they contain much in the way of decoration and artifacts that assist us in piecing together the story of the peoples and the chronology of their art. At first it is quite probable that the outer surface of the buildings was rather simply decorated, probably in molded stucco. From there the development in sculptured stone was rapidly passed through a period of low relief to one in which the decoration was sculpture almost in the full round and back again to a highly stylized low relief. As artists there are few peoples who have exceeded the Mayas in ability. Their repetition is in accord with the best tenets of modern art. Their use of perspective far exceeded that of

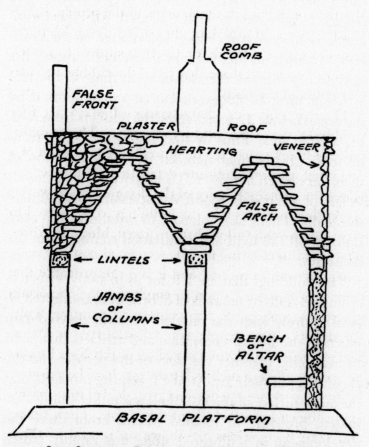

SOME STRUCTURAL DETAILS OF A MAYA 2-VAULT BUILDING

any of the great civilizations that developed around the Mediterranean and in the figuring of the profile, three-quarter face and full face they have never been exceeded. In general the decoration was applied to a thick veneer of trimmed stone that faced the rubble and masonry bulk of the walls.

There is only one characteristic of Maya art that troubles a twentieth century observer. Their abhorrence of blank spaces led them to fill every portion of a decorated area with minute detail that frequently obscures the principal figure of the decoration. However, everything indicates that the buildings were painted in vivid colors—red, yellow, brown, green, blue and white. Traces of this coloring may be seen on almost any monument or wall examined and it is quite probable that color was depended upon to emphasize the important objects in each panel. In addition to painting sculptured works these people were adept at frescos. Particularly is this true in the later cities of the New Empire where a number of such wall paintings have been found. From these too we can derive a great deal of information about the customs and life of the people. Their houses and their occupations are shown on several of them. Further enlightenment is gained from their books of which, unfortunately, only one or two remain to us. The zeal of Bishop Landa in stamping out the old religion and replacing it with Christianity led to the wholesale and practically total destruction of this type of art.

Almost every one of the temple buildings throughout

the region is raised above the level of the ground on a platform or pyramid varying in height from a few feet to almost a hundred. Some of these higher pyramids are terraced, others are not. Frequently, in order to give height to a building, a roof comb of no utility was built upon it. These were highly ornamented and represent a peculiarity found nowhere else on the American continents. Whether the *adornos* in these roof combs had a significance is not known. It is possible that in the coastal towns they may have been markers to advise strange seafaring ships of the town they were approaching. On the earlier buildings and on the rectangular monuments and pilasters are representations, life-size or greater, of warriors, priests and gods so completely executed that it is easy for us today to determine the special costumes of a city and the changes in styles as they took place.

With the Toltec invasion toward the close of the first Christian millenium marked changes occurred in the style of architecture. This is evidenced most strongly in the use of the timbered roof in smaller buildings and of rounded columns to support porticoes and colonnades. A curious remnant of a Toltec custom in the Valley of Mexico is found in the cemeteries of the Maya-Toltec cities. In their homeland where the Toltecs had an abundance of skulls from sacrificial victims they walled their cemeteries with fences made by stringing skulls on wooden poles and setting them up like a hedge. With no available supply of crania to satisfy this whim of the

Toltecs the Mayas built cemetery walls of stone upon which they engraved row upon row of skulls strung together on carved poles. It is probably because of the Toltecs that in the later cities the serpent motif is so prominent. This mode of decoration is not seen in the buildings of the Old Empire nor in the early buildings in eastern Yucatan.

Rather recently excavators have discovered a problem that adds to the many difficulties in studying and reconstructing the Maya buildings. Apparently as time went on, styles or architecture changed and temples became outmoded. In at least three cases we know that the builders merely filled up the old building with refuse, covered it and its platform with a complete new shell and built on top of the greatly enlarged pyramid a new temple. I believe the earliest example of this was discovered by Dr. Morley at Uaxactun. Two others are known as Chichen Itza where, while reconstructing the Temple of the Warriors, Mr. Earl Morris discovered an entombed temple in the pyramidal base of the building he was restoring; and only a few years ago I had the opportunity of being at hand while Señor Eduardo Martinez prospected and discovered a similarly buried temple within the pyramid of the Temple of Kukulcan at Chichen Itza.

With a style of architecture that is so varied and interesting and important it is to be expected that the lesser arts of the Maya people have been somewhat neglected. As potters they were exceeded on the American continents by only the Peruvians living along the coast. As might be expected their most beautiful and finished products were ceremonial ware. The service ware, as a matter of fact, is really quite inferior to much of the pottery that is found to the north. The study of debris carefully excavated from a cave near the ancient city of Pusilhá will lead probably to a far better knowledge of the pottery than we have today. This city seems to have been the ceramic center of the Maya empires. The ceremonial ware was made in a great variety of shapes and often beautifully decorated with painted designs that frequently depict a portion of a ceremony. A pot picked up some years ago on the southern border of the region occupied by these people illustrates a procession of priests and their acolytes leading an aged man to sacrifice. The draftmanship and ceramic technique shown on this pot rank with the best for all times. In addition to bowl and vase shapes and the usual run of zoömorphic figurines, the clay workers were highly adept at modeling images that have all the earmarks of portraiture.

Wood carving is another field in which these people excelled and lintels carved centuries ago from sapote wood have resisted the decay of ages so well that it is possible to decipher the glyphs on them. One thing that must be kept in mind about these people is that their crafts were carried on without the aid of metal tools. All their wood carving and stone sculpture was done with stone implements. As might be expected their workmanship in flint was of high rank. It is surpassed only by that of the Danes and the Egyptians. In one form of shaping they were nowhere excelled and that is in the manufacture of eccentric shapes, some of them geometric and some of them zoömorphic, representing a variety of animals and men so well executed that they are recognized without any difficulty.

The few metal objects that have been found in the Maya area are without a doubt pieces of trade goods that were brought in from the outside. The occasional gold trinkets are identical with those that are abundant in Costa Rica and we may well believe that area to be the source of these objects found in southern Mexico and Yucatan.

Almost more rare than gold are copper and natural bronze artifacts that were probably imported from Oaxaca in western Mexico. This region, too, probably supplied the jadeite that was so highly prized by these people. It is interesting to note the decline in the supply by the size of the pieces used through the time of the Maya people. At first large lumps were crudely shaped and carved and in the latest ruins only small beads and pendants are found.

As weavers the women were quite equal to the men in handicraft. Cloth was woven of cotton and sisal in strips about fifteen inches wide which were sewn together to form the garments of the people. As basket makers they were not so good. The surviving fragments of sisal bags and reed baskets and mats are of really low quality.

4

At the 19th International Congress of Americanists held in Washington in 1915 Dr. Morley proposed a division of Maya history into two general parts—the Old Empire and the New Empire. Since that time the evidence that has accrued has led students to consider that the division between the two is less sharp than formerly it was supposed to be. However, there are a great many characteristics that set apart Old Empire cities from New and it is just as well to retain the classification until the great basal area of the peninsula of Yucatan is explored thoroughly and its ruins studied. It is quite possible that when that work is completed the Old Empire cities will be found to intergrade rather uniformly into the New Empire. The experience of most of the archeologists of the early part of this century and during the last century was derived from the very heart of the Old Empire and the extreme northeastern fringe of the New Empire. In any cultural group of primitive peoples distances of 500 and 600 miles will cause to develop greatly different cultural characteristics in their remains. One of the most prominent of the differences between the Old and the New areas is the scarcity of initial series or Long Count dates in the latter region, there being only two at present deciphered, one at Chichen Itza and one at Tuluum. There are a great number of them in the Old Empire. This is evidence strongly in favor of the division. The lack of stelae bearing dates in the New Empire and the great number of them in the Old Empire is evidence of the same kind.

Dr. Teeple, in studying the glyphs preparatory to his great contribution on Maya astronomy, found that in the Old Empire three distinct phases were evidenced. The first was a Period of Independence during which time each city developed its own peculiar style of sculpture and hieroglyphics. This was followed by a Period of Unity when the system of glyph writing was uniform throughout the region. The second period lasted for several centuries and was then followed by what he calls the Period of Revolt that is recognizable by a gradual divergence in the characterization of the glyphs.

Little or nothing has been left us of the actual history of the Old Empire. All that we can do is interpret the ruins as they are today, having been deserted for a thousand years. Just what caused this desertion we do not know. Innumerable reasons have been given but none of them seems to fit. War, pestilence, climatic changes, shortage of food and superstition have been defended by this author or that but I doubt if any one reason has more than its author in defense of it. Nevertheless, the desertion did take place and the people moved to the northeast into the peninsula of Yucatan, a far less favorable place to live in, and left the magnificent cities to crumble before the advance of the tropical jungle.

Perhaps the most logical of all the explanations is the one most recently made. Several points must be emphasized as a preamble to this. The Old Empire region lies almost wholly in the Peten of Guatemala. This name is a Maya word denoting lake. There are some lakes in the region today but not enough to warrant such an appellation nor to have supplied the ancient communities with adequate water. In earlier time there must have been many more. In the second place, practically all the ruins stand on little rises of ground above the general level of the marshy jungle bottom. The ancient communities are rather close together and the region in the past must have supported a very large population, which must have necessitated extensive clearing of the jungle. Now let us suppose that the boggy lands of today were lakes in the old days, and that the communities were situated on the shores of these lakes. This fact might account for the region being called Peten. Extensive agriculture by the milpa method in this region of heavy rains would in time cause these important water ways to become clogged with silt. The stagnation of the water would breed swarms of noxious insects and deprive the natives of adequate channels for travel and commerce; further silting up would deprive them of potable water. Only abandonment of the region and a general migration could result. Dated monuments tell us of a rather wide spread desertion of the region over a comparatively short time. The explanation seems to fit the known facts and may well be the true one.

Archeologists grubbing around in these decayed cities

have amassed a wealth of information but all of it relates to the art and architecture. Indirectly, of course, we learn something of the habits and costumes of the people from the figures inscribed upon the monuments. Different cities are noted for different things just as they are today. Copan, in the far south, has an abundance of sculptured stelae, monuments that were erected to commemorate the closing of five-year periods. Tikal, in the lowland at the root of the peninsula of Yucatan, far exceeds all other cities in the wood carving that is left to us in the form of door lintels. Quirigua, on the Rio Motagua in Guatemala not far from Copan, is renowned for its extraordinary zoömorphic figures. Palenque, in the extreme northwest, is unsurpassed in its modeled stucco and engraved jade. The frontispiece of this volume is a restoration of a piece of Palenque stucco. Pusilhá, at the southern tip of British Honduras, is the home of the finest ceramics of the region and at Lubaantun, just to the north, great quantities of beautiful figurines are found. In the New Empire Chichen Itza, the great Holy City, has the largest of the ball courts.

Perhaps it would not be amiss at this point to describe a city from each of these areas. In the Old Empire Copan is one of the two really first class cities and we will use it. In the New Empire Chichen Itza is outstanding in many respects so it will be our representative late city.

Copan is situated in Honduras just across the border from Guatemala on the Rio Copan, a tributary of the

Rio Motagua. It is one of the most favorably situated of all the Maya cities as far as climate is concerned. Its elevation, about two thousand feet above sea level, raises it above the dank humid lowlands of the coastal plain and, although toward the end of the dry season it becomes rather hot in the middle of the day, the mornings and evenings are always cool. Water is abundant, there being an annual rainfall of about sixty inches. The surrounding country supports a dense verdant forest of many useful types of trees. The river valley is particularly fertile and even today is extensively farmed. The forest abounds with animals that may be used for food and there is nothing to indicate that the conditions today are better than they were during the time of the occupancy of the site.

Approaching the valley from the northwest, a little more than three miles before the main group of ruins is reached, the rough wagon-road from Zacapa zig-zags over the hills of decaying volcanic stone and skirts the edge of a small valley containing Hacienda Grande, one of the modern settlements along the Rio Copan. Here are ruins that probably formed a suburb of the main city in ancient times. Situated on the plaza is a single stone monument bearing a date, 9.10.19–15–0 (652 A. D.), thus placing the structures there at about the middle period of the development of Copan. Further along, situated on the crest of a hill about three miles from the main group, is evidence of considerable work. Several altars on a large leveled area with a retaining

wall running along its eastern edge are grouped near
what is known locally as the western Piedra Pintada,
archeologically as Stela 10. This, along with Number 12
some four and a half miles to the east, has been thought
of as a giant sun dial and it has been suggested by Dr.
Spinden that it was used to set the beginning of the
Maya year and to mark the equinox. However, ob-
servations taken on March 8, 1916 by Mr. Carpenter
on the Carnegie Institution Expedition and turned over
to Professor Willson of the Harvard Astronomical Department show that in that year, at any rate, the setting
sun was in line with the two stelae about twenty days
distant from the equinox. Whether there has been sufficient shift since the monuments were erected to account for this is doubtful. Another point of evidence
that does not follow in line with the sun dial idea is
that the dates inscribed upon the stelae do not corre-
spond with the eight possible dates for the beginning
of the Maya year which was governed, it is believed,
by the equinox.

Traveling on down the hill and around through a
little side valley the visitor soon approaches one of the
great centers of Copan near the present village bearing
the same name. Here are many remains of a large settlement. The present village plaza occupies the large plaza
of the old city and is surrounded by a number of pyramids and mounds that are the remains of temples. Scattered about are a great many stelae and altars bearing
inscriptions that have been deciphered by Dr. Morley.

Here are grouped the most ancient of all the monuments at Copan. The earliest bears the date 9.1.10–0–0 (465 A. D.) and, with the exception of one, the latest was erected in 9.9.0–0–0 (613 A. D.). This exception is an altar situated near the northeast corner of the remains and is inscribed with the date 9.17.12–5–17 (782 A. D). Across the top is sculptured a crocodile decorated along its backbone with a single band of glyphs. On the sides of the block are engraved glyphs and human figures which resemble those of the famous Altar Q which is believed to represent a Congress of astronomers and will be described more completely further on. The long gap between the date on this monument and all the others at the site seems to indicate that it was deserted for several hundred years and then reoccupied just before the city was abandoned.

Crossing the Rio Sesesmil the traveler passes a small group of altars and stelae that were erected during the middle period of the occupancy of the city. Just beyond this small group the road branches, the right hand fork crossing the flat river valley to the main structure of Copan and the left skirting the ancient quarries and going on to the town of Santa Rita where there are a number of mounds and a single monument bearing the date 9.11.0–0–0 (652 A. D.). The main structure of the region is situated directly upon the banks of the river. Apparently during the time of occupancy the river was considerably to the southeast of where it now lies. During the interim it has swung northward and cut a huge slice from the corner of the great mound exposing an archeological cross section that is possibly the largest in the world—over 100 feet high and over 300 feet long. This main region is composed of five large plazas surrounded by pyramids, temples and platforms. Whether any of the great stone structures were used as dwelling places is not certainly known. However, there is no reason to deny the possibility. In the New Empire region we know this to have occurred. At the north end is a great plaza with many dated stelae and altars. To the west, the north and the east of this are terraces that supported small pyramids capped with temples. In the opening left at the south another pyramid was erected. Opposing this plaza and facing the north is an extraordinary terrace over 200 feet wide and about 60 feet high. To the east of this terrace and facing the west is the famous Hieroglyphic Stairway that mounts to a four-room temple built on top of a partial pyramid. The inscription giving the name to it contains over 2,500 individual glyphs. The Stairway itself is about twenty-five feet wide and is flanked by broad balustrades over three feet wide. Unfortunately, the ravages of time have so dismembered it that only ten complete steps and parts of five others were found in place when the slope was cleared. The balustrade was ornamented at intervals of every five steps with the so-called period symbols. At regular intervals along the center line of the Stairway from top to bottom were heroic carved figures of seated humans. Of these only one was found in place, the collapse of the

ACROPOLIS OF COPAN

(Courtesy, Carnegie Institution, Washington, D. C.)

Stairway having carried the others to the bottom. The figures measure about six feet in height in the sitting position.

From the platform at the head of the Stairway where the temple is situated one can easily walk about on what has been called the Acropolis. At present there is no other evidence of access to this high platform. However, Garcia de la Palacio, who wrote in 1576, described a grand stairway descending to the river. It is quite probable that this approach was destroyed by the stream shifting in its course. On the Acropolis is situated Altar Q that has been described by several as commemorating a conference of astronomers at Copan. If this is true, it may be called the first meeting of the American Association for the Advancement of Science. The altar is a rectangular block of stone resting on four roughly spherical supports. All four sides and the top are fully engraved. The top bears thirty-six glyph signs of which several compose important dates which also occur four times at the neighboring city of Quirigua. Morley's transcriptions of the dates led him to believe that the altar was dedicated at the close of 9.17.5–0–0 on the day 6 *Ahau* 13 *Kayab*. The figures on the sides of the stone are in groups of four. On the front panel they are paired facing the middle. On the side panels the figures face the front of the stone. Those of the back, however, are placed in such a way as to form a continuous band with those on the left side. Each of the figures is seated cross-legged on blocks of glyphs and holds in the hand in front of the face a three-parted wand which may represent an astronomical instrument. As a matter of fact, it resembles closely an astrolabe. The breasts of several are decorated with distinctive and curious grotesque masks. Each is wearing a peculiar headdress composed of a conical turban with three loops at the top and two trailing ribbons behind.

It is unfortunate that so much of Copan is in utter ruin. It must have been a wonderful city. It was abandoned apparently some time toward the end of the 8th century but it was again used by the Mayas for defense against the Spaniards.

For the casual visitor and for the student of pre-Columbian history too Chichen Itza, the great city of the New Empire, is probably the best of all Maya cities to visit. There through the long continued efforts of the Carnegie Institution and the Department of Antiquities of the Mexican Government many of the ancient buildings have been restored to something of their former grandeur. Trails have been cleared and a rest house erected.

The city was settled in 462 A. D. according to the Book of Chilam Balam, one of the few chronicles left us written by Mayas. It is quite probable that the area known as South Chichen Itza was the one first occupied. There the Carnegie Institution made its first restoration of a Maya building. The Temple of the Two Lintels is probably one of the choicest gems of Maya architecture that has been left to us. What it was called by the Mayas

TEMPLE OF THE TWO LINTELS

Photo. by Laura Gilpin, Colorado Springs, Colo.

and what its use was we do not know. Archeologists and travelers have given names to the Maya buildings to suit their fancies. In late years there has been a real attempt made to study its possible uses before naming a building. However, many were merely arbitrarily named.

This little building, situated about three miles south of the great city, was a tumbled ruin with only a small portion of the south wall standing when the archeologists and engineers set about their task. Laboriously they examined the stones in the positions in which they had fallen and from the small standing portion received enough of an idea to enable them to replace practically every stone they found. The lower part of the walls is smooth and undecorated. It is quite probable that in the time of its occupancy this was colored red. Today it is gleaming white limestone. As has been explained previously, the peculiar construction of the Maya arch required a very deep roof. This roof band is ornamented with alternate panels representing vertical logs on the one hand and a latticework of carved stone on the other. The four corners are further decorated with grotesque masks of Itzamna, the Rain God, whose curiously hooked nose, filed teeth and square earplugs are characteristics by which his mask may be identified easily.

Between this building and Old Chichen Itza, scattered through the brush and jungle, are numerous small mounds each the remains of a little temple. It is not until the wanderer reaches Old Chichen that he gets among buildings built close together and, for Maya ruins, in a tolerably good state of preservation. Among this group of temples is situated the Temple of the Initial Inscription the lintel stone of which bears the only complete date in Chichen Itza—10.2.10–0–0 (620 A. D.). It is quite probable that the present temple and lintel stone are not in the original position or shape. A crypt just to the west is built of stones that were taken from another building and without a doubt the lintel stone came from it too. Its date is much too early for the type of columns that support it. These are splendid examples of the so-called Atlantean figures which were brought into the region by the Toltecs probably during the 10th century. In this area we see the greatest number of buildings showing the fusion of Toltec and Maya cultures. Just to the south of the Temple of the Initial Inscription is a quadrangle opening to the east, the entrance to which is guarded by two such figures of heroic size. The presence of *phalloi* in the walls of the chambers in this quadrangle is one of the rare indications of phallic worship found in North America. To the northwest of the quadrangle are several small temples with square pilasters and one or two with round columns. The square pilaster is typically Maya while the round column is Toltec.

Going north from this group of buildings you approach the area that was occupied just before the Conquest. Here are situated, among other important and

interesting buildings, the nunnery or Casa de las Monjas, the Caracol or observatory and the Temple of the
Wall Panels. The Casa de las Monjas is to the south of
what probably was the great plaza when this area represented the highest development at Chichen. Although
the building has the appearance of being several stories
high it is really not so but consists of several tiers built
on what is thought to be a solid core. The walls of this
structure are probably the most highly ornate in all
Chichen Itza. The lattice work design is particularly
well executed and occupies a great deal of the space below the roof band. The deep panel trimming the sides of
the roof is made up of a continuous band of Itzamna
masks. A broad steep stairway leads from the plaza to the
small temple space on the top of the pile. To the north
and a little east is the observatory, the only standing circular Maya building that is known. It is placed upon a
terrace about twelve feet high and approached by a
broad flight of stairs on the west side. The construction
of the building with its spiral staircase inside the tower
and the numerous slits through the thick walls have led
students to believe that it was used by the astronomer-
priests in determining the position of heavenly bodies.
Between these two buildings on the east side of the
plaza is the Temple of the Wall Panels, a lovely structure that has been excavated and partially restored. It
derives its name from the sculptured panels on the
otherwise plain walls.

From the observatory and from the Casa de las Monjas paved roads lead through the brush to the most modern area in the city and beyond it to a sacred well. Traveling this ancient highway you pass the Temple to the High Priest which is a pyramid erected over the crypt that held the ashes of some high dignitary of Maya times. This crypt is in a natural cavern in the limestone and it is quite probable that it connects with the cave at the water level of the Cenote Xtoloc, one of the wells that probably supplied the people with drinking water. The road emerges from the bush nowadays just to the west of the great pyramid. This has been restored to a great extent through the efforts of the Mexican Government. Señor Martinez has left two of the faces in the condition in which they were when the brush had been cleared from the surfaces. The other two, the west and the north, have been restored completely. The pyramid is made up of a succession of terraces and up each of the four faces broad stairways lead. The balustrades are wide and terminate on the ground level in exquisitely sculptured serpent heads. The broad platform at the top serves as the base for the Temple of Kukulcan, our old friend Quetzlcoatl of the Mexican area. On one of the door jambs of this temple is engraved in very low relief what may be considered a portrait bas-relief of that dignitary. It shows him with a long beard, an adornment quite strange among any of the branches of the Asiatic people. It is here that we can see also loop holes cut into the stone through which heavy cords could be stretched barring the entrances. Looking down to the east the observer sees the magnificent Temple of the Warriors restored by Mr. Earl Morris. The temple itself is built upon a lower but larger terraced pyramid banded with friezes of warriors and animals. It is approached by a steep stairway on the west. Surrounding it and extending around a huge plaza to the south is the Colonnade of a Thousand Columns. Those columns directly west of the Temple of the Warriors are square and on each of the four faces bear bas-reliefs of warriors, priests and gods. Those to the south are all circular and represent an earlier structure. At the extreme south of the colonnade are the recently restored Mercado and Escuela. The buildings on the east side of the plaza are still tree-capped mounds of debris.

To the west from the top of the great pyramid the Temple of the Tigers and the great ball court fill the view. The cemetery with its beautiful carving becomes almost insignificant. The ball court is the largest one known and has just been restored completely along with its appurtenant temple, the Temple of the Tigers, by the Mexican Government. Here the forerunner of basket ball was played. High on the smooth playing walls opposed to each other are a pair of stone rings set vertically. The game was played on the paved court by teams of seven men using a solid live-rubber ball that weighed eight or ten pounds. A goal was scored when that ball was tossed through the ring some eighteen feet above the playing level. The reward to a player for such a feat was that he might claim any article of clothing from the spectators. It is said that when experts played the game they did not use their hands but obeyed rules somewhat like those of modern soccer. At the north end of the playing field is a little temple with perfect acoustic properties that I have dubbed the "Temple of the Orators," for a person standing there speaking in a normal voice can be heard perfectly 600 feet away at the other end of the court.

Turning to the cemetery lying just east of the ball court we see the evidence of the basic difference between the Mayas and the Toltecs. Among the latter people it was customary to wall in the cemetery with row upon row of human skulls driven together on poles of wood. As has already been mentioned the Maya method for making up for the lack of victims' skulls was to carve them of stone. Adjacent to that plot of ground are what I believe to be the remains of the Funiary Temples. One of them, because of the predominant decoration in the frieze, is called the Temple of the Eagles.

Going north again along the ancient paved highway one soon reaches the Sacred Well. The little temple on its south side from which the sacrificial victims were tossed is reduced to ruins and only traces of it can be seen. The well itself is about 150 feet in diameter and there is a sheer drop of over 70 feet to the level of the water. In years of great drouth it was the Maya custom to offer to the Rain God a new bride at the well and it seems evident that the well was used by all the cities throughout eastern Yucatan. The story goes that the most beautiful of the Maya daughters were sent to live at the Casa de las Monjas where they were trained as priestesses. When a sacrifice to the Rain God was necessary or, as they would put it, a new bride was necessary one of the girls was selected from this group studying at the Casa de las Monjas. With a great deal of pomp she was prepared for her coming wedding. The day previous to the great celebration called for the preparation of her body. This is described in part in the very recently translated Gomesta Manuscript * which contains the following formula "for making a paint for the goddess who was to be sacrificed in the Cenote; it is composed of the following; gum of the Cedrosa (cedar), tiger's fat, certain plants that yield a dark green color, and are called in Maya *Cholipia;* and from these leaves they extract the resins, put them to boil until parboiled; afterwards they painted the unfortunate goddess so that she might not swell up in the Cenote. This painting was prescribed for all those sacrificed, and they put it on a day before the sacrifice, and carried her in a procession with music and religious songs." It is quite probable that much of the ceremony was carried on in the large paved plaza in front of the great pyramid. From there the fateful procession moved slowly down the road that is still used in traveling to the well to the little temple on the brink of the abyss. Other chronicles

* Dr. Franz Blom has studied this manuscript critically and declares it to be a counterfeit. Dr. William Gates insists that it is genuine. The argument of Dr. Blom seems convincing to me.

tell us that if the girl survived the fall and managed to live in the water until sundown she was rescued and venerated as an actual goddess. This was also considered to be a sign that the Rain God was satisfied with his last bride and the Mayas would just have to wait until he got ready to let it rain.

About thirty years ago Mr. Edward Thompson explored the well for the Peabody Museum at Harvard University using diver's equipment. He brought up from the bottom many skeletons of young girls and a wealth of trinkets that they had worn to their doom, thus proving clearly the tales that had been handed down over three hundred years.

CHAPTER SIX

THE AZTECS

1

DR. SPINDEN in his compact handbook of the civilizations in Mexico has drawn a very apt analogy between the high civilizations there and those on the northern edge of the Mediterranean. Just as the Greeks were the artistic intellectual group and the Romans the warlike and practical nation so the Mayas were the center of intellect and the Aztecs a race of warriors. The Toltec reign which was responsible for a great many of the monumental ruins in the Valley of Mexico and to the south ended about 1220 when the barbaric Nahual tribes began to raid their more civilized neighbors. It was only a short time until the Aztecs practically controlled the Valley of Mexico and in 1225 their first nomadic ruler was proclaimed. For a century and a half these barbaric warriors who claimed to have come from the Island of Atlan roamed the country conquering cities and tribes. It was not until Acamapichtli ascended to the rulership in 1376 that the dynasty of "sedentary emperors" began. The center of the government of the Aztec nation was always located on the lake outside of the present city of Mexico—first at Texcoco and later

at Tenochtitlan, the city that was leveled by the Spaniards and forms the foundation upon which Mexico
City arose. The reign of the Aztec rulers came to a close
in 1521 just one year after the men of Cortez met with
these barbaric warriors. The last true ruler was Moctezuma the Second who ruled from 1502 to 1520. During
the time that he was held hostage by the Spaniards the
titulary ruler was Cuitlahua who before the end of the
year was succeeded by Cuauhtemoc whose reign also
lasted but a few months.

It was because of the organization of the Aztec
empire, if we may call it such, that the Spanish were
able to reduce this powerful group of warriors in so
short a time. Three things contributed to the downfall
of the native empire. First, because of a legend the
white men were allowed to land and were presented
with gifts including gold which whetted their hunger
for the precious metal. The myth was that of Kukulcan,
or as he was known in this region, Quetzalcoatl, who is
reputed to have said, when he was banished and retired
to the coast near Vera Cruz, that he would return in the
future upon the wings of a great white bird from out
of the east. The Spanish ships with their huge white
sails coming from Cuba and the light-skinned bearded
men dressed in their burnished armor fulfilled this
prophecy to the word; and so the arrival of the strangers
to the shore of Mexico was welcomed as the return of
one of their greatest of gods. The second reason for the
comparatively easy victory of the Spaniards was that the

method of subjugation practiced by the Aztecs led to considerable discontent among their vassal neighbors. This gave Cortez many native troops as allies who knew the country and the local methods of warfare. The third and almost as powerful reason was that the Aztec religion required innumerable individuals for human sacrifice and war was waged primarily to keep up this supply. It was the aim of every Aztec soldier to capture, not to kill. On the other hand, it was the aim of every Spanish warrior to kill, not to capture. The long distance fighting equipment of the Spaniards with killing in mind was far more effective than the hand to hand battle of the Aztecs. If the two groups had met on even ground in the same type of warfare there is not the slightest doubt that the Spaniards would never have gained the upper hand in Mexico.

The social organization of these last Mexicans was such that every man at some time during his life served in the army or was a priest, so that the fighting forces that rallied under Moctezuma the Second comprised every able-bodied man in the empire. This citizenry was organized geographically into twenty groups that might be termed clans. They were called *calpolli* which means great houses. I do not believe that such clans were made up of individuals all of the same lineage but that the name "great houses" was derived from the meeting house in which the elders gathered once every twenty day month to settle the local affairs of the neighborhood. To that extent the Aztec government was dem-

ocratic. However, the actual ruler was far more autocratic than democratic. As in England and in Russia
before the revolution, the ruler was the head of both
state and church. The Aztec ruler far more closely resembled the Czar than the King of England in the
powers he held over his people.

Succession to the rulership is rather interesting. It
was not truly hereditary in that it did not invariably
pass from father to son. Upon the death of the chieftain,
his successor was chosen from the group of males in his
family, immediate or distant. The one selected was he
who was thought to be the most capable war leader.
Thus, although the rulership was not hereditary it was
restricted to a single family.

The laws of the land were extraordinarily strict and
death was the punishment for almost every crime
whether it be a major one or a minor one, whether it be
a civil crime or a social one. The other punishment was
slavery which, from our point of view, seems to be severe
but actually was not. Slaves could own property and be-
longings. In general the state of slavery was rather one
of working for an individual without pay for a part of
the time than the bondage such as we in our country
had before the Proclamation of Emancipation. Frequently a man would sell himself into slavery to pay his
debts and it was possible to buy one's way out of the
hands of an owner. Frequently children were sold for
a period of time and during the service might return to
their parents for any length of time provided a substi-

tute was sent to serve in their places. Upon the death of an owner the slaves were frequently freed according to his will. If this did not occur, they were the property of his heirs. It was not at all infrequent that a widower married one of his slaves and her progeny were treated as the rightful heirs to the property of the man upon his death. Occasionally the slaves were used in certain sacrificial ceremonies. It was, however, the prisoners of war that supplied most of the victims for these bloody rites.

Warfare among the Aztecs as among the Mayas was a ceremonial affair. It was really war by appointment. Two groups with a grievance would decide to meet in the field of battle at the border of their lands. Each army would draw up on its own territory and if one arrived before the other it merely made camp and awaited the coming of its enemy. The night before the day set for the attack was consumed in ceremony and in the morning when the symbols for war were hoisted by both generals the conflict began. Among the Aztecs as among the Mayas, the aim was to get captives rather than to kill. Although the equipment of the soldier was deadly and many were slain, by far the greater number were captured and reserved for sacrifice. Each warrior went to battle covered with a heavy cotton quilting and a shield made in such fashion that it could be rolled up when not in use. Bows and arrows, spears and spear throwers and vicious wooden swords edged with razor-sharp fragments of obsidian constituted the implements of strife. When the armies returned to their homes the captives were imprisoned in wooden cages and well treated. Apparently it was felt to be an honor to be sacrificed to the gods.

Just as today, commercial expansion was the reason for many of the wars that were waged. Instead of commerce following the flag, the flag followed commerce. The Aztec business men spread their influence throughout all Mexico, south to Honduras and north to the Pueblos of Arizona and New Mexico. They traveled in caravans as a protection against warlike peoples upon whose land they trespassed. Occasionally a minor ruler taxed these caravans for the use of his trails. Such tribute was always given grudgingly and when the merchant felt that he was being oppressed he called upon his government to wage war upon his oppressor in order that his goods might be transported through the region without toll. That is not unlike the state of affairs today.

The market places of the Aztec cities that these commercial travelers supplied were much as the market squares in Mexico today where practically every want of the people may be satisfied. Everything from charcoal and firewood to the most beautiful of fabrics and ceramics was available. Foods from the sea, from the hot lowlands, from the cold uplands, charms of all kinds were laid out on market day to appease the whims of the population. Trade was carried on in general by the barter method. That is, people from the outlying districts would bring in their produce and exchange it for luxuries brought from distant lands. Among the wealthy people who lived in the cities barter was out of the question. So they bought what they wished with "money." The smallest denomination of this money was a single cocoa bean. This type of currency was used for small purchases although sacks containing 400 and 8000 of the beans could be used in paying larger bills; but that would be something like paying for an automobile with dimes or quarters. Pieces of cotton cloth served as a medium of exchange and these were a little bit more valuable than cocoa beans. For extremely expensive purchases tiny nuggets or flakes of gold packed in perfectly transparent duck quills were used for money. Biart, in his summary of Aztec life, also mentions tin in small irregular pieces as having monetary value. If this is so, I would be interested to know where the tin came from—whether it was the product of Bolivia and Peru and thus came to Mexico through trade with the Incas.

2

Of the arts and crafts by far the most important among the Aztecs was agriculture for they, like all of the other groups of American civilized Indians, had an agricultural background. Within the empire itself the land was owned by either the nobility or the community, the *calpolli*. The average villager was allowed to farm all the land he could but if any fields lay fallow for more than two years they reverted to the community and were given to more industrious farmers. This land, to all intents, was the property of the man so long as he worked it and lived in the village. However, he could not sell it nor transfer it to another except at his death when his sons inherited the land. The estates of the nobility could be sold. Most of them were areas that had been granted by the ruler as rewards for services during campaigns and many of them were situated in conquered land.

The crops that were raised depended upon the region. In the lower hot lands cocoa, cotton and maguey were the principal products. In the colder uplands corn, amaranth and some maguey were grown. In addition to these great crops there were many of lesser importance, the variety we call today truck products. Tomatoes, sweet potatoes, beans, many varieties of squash and peppers are a few of the important vegetables that were in daily use. As has been already stated, cocoa served as a medium of exchange; therefore those lowland estates that could produce this bean were highly prized by the aristocracy and guarded zealously from invasion. The cotton was the source of the clothing of all the better class people. The lowly ones, however, resorted to the coarse tough fabrics of the maguey and sisal. In addition to supplying material for fabrics the maguey yielded an intoxicating beverage that is still very popular in Mexico—pulque. This was made by fermenting the sweet juices that dripped from slashes made in the heavy fleshy leaves of the plant. Peyote, a powerful drug, was made from the dried flowers of a certain type of cactus.

This substance was important in many of the ceremonies of the people. It was eaten with honey and caused hallucinations which gave the eater false ideas of his strength and bravery. Two animals were raised for food. There were several varieties of dog that were carefully tended, fed upon corn products, raw and cooked meats and fattened for the table. Flocks of turkeys were raised for the same purpose.

These birds also supplied feathers for decoration. Robes of cotton had sewed to them the smaller and softer bird feathers. The metallic ones found on the turkey were admirable for such a purpose. At Tenochtitlan and probably at other great centers great aviaries were kept where birds were raised especially to supply feathers for these robes. In the list given by the Conquistadors is the Quetzal bird. If this bird really was kept in captivity by the Aztecs they succeeded in doing something that not even the best equipped zoölogical garden of today has been able to do. The finest of these feathered robes were made so carefully that each feather overlapped the quill of another so the finished product showed only the soft colorful plumes.

Fabrics were dyed, too, in order to give them variety and beauty. Many vegetable substances were called upon in this art. From the coast came a tiny mollusk, *Purpura patula,* which when properly treated yielded up a beautiful dye. Such purple dyed robes were worn only by the elect of the community. Another animal, this time an insect, was used for coloring matter. It is the tiny coccid that lives on cactus and exudes a deep red dye, cochineal. It is said that with careful tending three crops of cochineal bugs could be raised in a year on a single patch of cactus but that only the first and second produced really first class dye. There were two methods used in putting a design of color into fabric. The simplest was to weave threads of different color. The other, much less frequently practiced, was tie-dyeing and it was done just as it is today, by wrapping portions of the cloth so tightly with thread or cord that they could not take up the dye solution when the entire piece was plunged into it.

The work of the Aztec lapidaries is startling when one considers the crude materials with which these craftsmen worked. They used a great many substances in their art—quartz, fluorite, turquoise, jadeite and even emeralds, besides innumerable pretty little pebbles that today would be scorned by a jeweler. These substances were used for making pendants and beads, amulets of all kinds and plugs for the nose, the lip and the ear. Occasionally a large piece was worked into an ornament for the household of some lord or the ruler himself. There is in the British Museum a replica of a human skull beautifully worked from a huge clear quartz crystal. We know very little of the techniques employed by these ancient jewelers. However, most of this work was probably done by grinding an abrasive with a bone tool or a piece of wood onto the surface of the stone to be worked. Although most of the turquoise used came probably

WOODEN DRUM FROM TENANGO
(Courtesy, Dept. of Publicity, the Mexican Government)

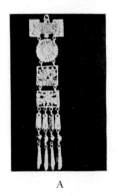

A

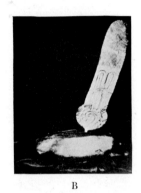

B

C

D

A, CAST GOLD PENDANT   B, GOLD PLUME AND CROWN
C, CARVED BONE BATONS   D, CAST GOLD BREASTPLATE AND MASK

MONTE ALBAN

(Courtesy, Dept. of Publicity, the Mexican Government)

great many interesting architectural features in addition to the temples. Great causeways, sometimes thirty feet high, were built across the low marshy land surrounding the Lake Texcoco. Aqueducts fully as marvelous as those built by the Caesars brought fresh water from the mountains far to the west of the city. The floating islands of Xochmilco were made by heaping earth upon great rafts. These wandered about the lake and were used for horticultural purposes for, in addition to a market for utilitarian produce, there were great flower markets in the Aztec cities. As among all civilizations with highly developed religious structures, the homes of the common people were simple and crude. From the Spanish chroniclers we learn that the Aztec yeomanry lived in wattle houses with thatched roofs and mud plastered walls, quite similar to those one sees today in the poorer towns in Mexico.

3

The religion of the Aztecs was a polytheism that seemed to be on the verge of changing to a monotheism. The pantheon contained hundreds of deities but the idea of there being a single power that controlled everything and was master over the lesser gods already had considerable support among the aristocracy. That All-Powerful God was called Tezcatlipoca. This deity had reached the point of being considered omnipotent and omnipresent. He was the most powerful of all the gods and led them back to earth on their annual return during the twelfth month of the eighteen month year of the Aztecs. He was the patron of the great schools for young warriors, a leader of the agricultural gods among whom he figured as both the God of Drouth and of Plenty and he was all-powerful in regard to life of both humans and gods, having the power to give or take it away.

Two other deities were almost as important in a general way as Tezcatlipoca. The holiest of these was Quetzalcoatl whose downfall mythology ascribes to the god just described. It is difficult to separate the god mythology from actual history in the case of the "Feathered Serpent." It is rather definitely understood now that there was a ruling Toltec by that name who played a great part in the conquest and Mexicanization of Yucatan and the Mayas. In the period just previous to the Spanish Conquest Quetzalcoatl still played a leading role in the religion of the southernmost people grouped together as the Aztecs. He was the leading god of the Toltecs. In the Aztec pantheon he was the Wind God and as such had considerable to do with the rainfall and clouds that controlled the crops. It is curious that the ancient myth established the date 1 *Acatl* as the beginning day of years particularly important in the worship of Quetzalcoatl. That was done because he was the lord of the planet Venus and the day on which the Venus cycle was supposed to have started was 1 *Acatl*. The myth stated that upon his banishment to the lowlands along the Gulf of Mexico Quetzalcoatl promised to re-

A   B

C

A, COATLICUE—GODDESS OF EARTH
B, XOCHIPILLI—GODDESS OF FLOWERS
C, XIUHCOATL—ESSENCE OF NEW FIRE
(Courtesy, Dept. of Publicity, the Mexican Government)

turn to the Mexicans in a year 1 *Acatl*. He said that upon his return he would approach the coast on a huge white-winged bird and would be wearing clothing bearing crosses. Cortez arrived in his white-sailed galleons in a year with a beginning date 1 *Acatl*. Is there any wonder that the superstitious Mexicans believed at first that his arrival was the return of one of their most beloved gods, the deity who was supposed to have introduced so many of their advances in culture?

The third of the rather general gods was Huitzilopochtli. According to the myths he was an early Aztec leader who died before the founding of Tenochtitlan and was deified later. His accoutrements in statues and codices indicate that he was the God of Hunting and through it probably a war god. In his honor the Mexican priests frequently sacrificed as many as five hundred captives in a single festival.

The lesser gods can be divided into groups whose particular domains were the various industries and occupations of the people. Primary among these are the agricultural gods and the sky gods. It is difficult to draw a sharp line between these two groups since many of the sky gods such as the Tlalocs were powerful in the agricultural ceremonies because of the great influence the weather has upon crops. The most evident characteristic of the worship of this pantheon is what appears to us to be its great brutality and bloodiness. A conservative estimate would be that in each of the principal cities eight hundred to one thousand men, women and

children were sacrificed each year. To our way of think-
ing, such a destruction of humanity is highly repulsive
yet, when it is considered that the Aztec modes of warfare were such that prisoners were taken rather than
enemies killed and that the major number of the sacrificial victims was drawn from among these prisoners,
the bloodshed does not seem so great as in a single battle between the armies of our more civilized and cul-
tured nations. There is considerable evidence that
death by sacrifice to the warriors of the Valley of Mexico was thought of as a high honor, possibly considered
in a better light by them than death on the battlefield
by the rank and file of a modern army.

The sequence of feasts and sacrifices was regulated
closely by the calendar which is a derivation of the more
complex Maya calendar that has already been discussed. The prime difference in the two systems is that
the Aztecs lacked a Long Count and used only the short
fifty-two-year cycle. As far as any individual person was
concerned, this would be adequate, for rarely would
one live through more than one cycle; just as today
the use of a year number within a century, such as '35
for 1935, is perfectly adequate for every day procedure.
The short period of 260 days which formed a sort of
sacred sequence was called the *Tonalamatl* and corresponds to the Maya period of the same name in both
length and structure, being twenty day signs running
concurrently with thirteen numbers. The day name and
number in this cycle was used for purposes of augury,

for protecting the course of a person's life or for the success of an enterprise. Travelers and war leaders paid strict attention to the suitability of the day in this calendar before setting out upon a venture. The true calendar corresponds fairly well with the solar year. It is like the Maya *haab* and was made up of a period of eighteen months of twenty days and closed with five nameless days.

During each of these calendar months special feasts were held in veneration of one or more of the gods. Descriptions of each of these eighteen principal feasts or celebrations would be a gory repetition of religious murder. In general there was a similarity to each other in all the ceremonies. However, each one would have its characteristic peculiarity. For instance those ceremonies held for the gods of rain during the months when rain was needed were accompanied by much wailing and crying, I suppose with the idea in mind of demonstrating to the gods what the people wanted. In the case of prayers to the rain gods when no rain was wanted it was considered extremely unfortunate if any tears were shed. In general after the preliminary ceremonies the victim of the sacrifice was carried to a stone altar over which he was bent backward and held in place by minor priests. The officiating priest then ripped open the chest cavity with an obsidian knife and snatched the still beating heart from within the body. This organ was held up to the sun and to the four directions, then cast into a special receptacle. The blood draining from it was collected and daubed on the images and altars of the god being venerated. The body of the victim was tossed from the pyramid where the sacrifice took place to the crowd below. It was then hacked into pieces and eaten as a part of the ceremony. Although but a few weeks went by each year without the Aztec populace indulging in bits of human flesh for food they cannot be considered cannibalistic since the act was performed more as a communion than as an act of sustenance. In some of the ceremonies, those held to the gods of agriculture and particularly the maize gods, the victim was decapitated to indicate the gathering of a crop. Xipe was a god to whom a curious sacrifice was made. His victims, after their heads had been removed, were skinned and the removed pelt worn for a period of twenty days by a minor priest. After this the priest went through an absolution ceremony and the captor of the prisoner who had been sacrificed performed a penance. Because the flayed skins soon assumed a golden yellow color the goldsmith guild adopted Xipe as their patron god and performed sacrifices to him in the second month of the Aztec year.

Among some of the agricultural ceremonies there was still evidence of fertility rites during which the gods were instructed in the method of producing new life.

The great accumulations of skulls and human bones that resulted from such wholesale slaughter as occurred during many of the ceremonies led to their use in fencing off the sacred burial ground, the *Tzompantli*. It was

the lack of such accumulations that made it necessary
for the Maya to carve skulls from stone for the *Tzompantli* that were instituted after their conquest by the
Toltecs. Several of the rites that were common to the
earlier civilizations are to be found in the Aztec rit-
ual. It was the discovery of baptism, communion and
confession and the use of the cross by these Indians that
led the Spaniards to believe that at some time in the
past they had been Christianized and were at that time
backsliders and therefore should be punished severely.

4

What with important ceremonies being held during
every twenty-day month and several minor ones, the
average Aztec's time was well filled with his religion.
However, there is evidence that at times he could relax
and did so. This was done by indulging in a series of
games some of which, to be sure, had a quasi-religious
significance. The most exciting of these and one that
derived from the Maya area after the conquest by the
Toltecs is the great ball game that has been described.
This was played with exactly the same rules as in Yucatan. The ball court was laid out similarly even to the
skull medallions that marked the ends of the playing
zones. Probably the most often indulged in recreation
was gambling. This was carried on whenever possible.
There was heavy betting on the outcome of the ball
game, the peasantry offering the products of their land

and crafts, the aristocracy gambling with jewels and works of art. A game something like dice played with beans painted black on one side and white on the other seems to have been quite a favorite and the old accounts tell us how the players offered sacrifices to their dice and pleaded with them just as the crap shooter of today does.

More closely related to the religion than out-and-out gambling were the dances. Generally these were highly formalized and frequently introductory to some temple ceremony. Usually the sexes danced separately. However, in some of the agricultural and fertility celebrations there was mixed dancing that occasionally became obscene. One of the most curious of the dances is one that is called by the Spaniards *volador*. I don't know the Aztec name for it. A stout pole was erected in the plaza atop of which was a small flat platform. The four dancers climbed the pole and went through an elaborate gesture dance high in the air above the crowd. When this was completed they seized ropes that had been twisted about the pole and after attaching themselves firmly to these dove from their platform and were whirled about the pole as the ropes unwound. It is said that the preparation was so careful that the fliers each made exactly thirteen revolutions before they reached the ground. Thus the four of them would count up the fifty-two years of the calendar cycle.

The younger people were kept out of mischief in school. From about the age of eight both boys and girls attended schools of either a public or boarding type.

Here they were thoroughly grounded in the language, in the rituals of the many feasts that were held each year and the boys were taught the art of war and the various crafts that were carried on by the people. The girls' higher education included the womanly crafts. During the years of attendance at school it was the duty of the girls to take care of the temples, to weave the cloth used in their decoration and as clothing for the priesthood. If any of these vestals had not married by the time she was twenty-two years old she remained the rest of her life as a nun, devoting her time to the instruction of the younger girls and to the care of some particular temple. The instructors in the boys' schools were of the priesthood who were among the few people that could read and write the ideography of the time.

Of the hundreds of "books" that must have been in existence at the time of the Spanish Conquest only thirteen or fourteen are known today, although many out-and-out counterfeits have been "found" and foisted upon unsuspecting bibliophiles. Of this small number of codices only two remain in the New World, one in Mexico and one in the United States. Those in the Old World were doubtlessly a part of Cortez' loot which he sent back as examples of what these new people he had just discovered were capable of doing. By far the major number of the Aztec volumes that fell into the hands of the Spaniards were destroyed by the priests as works of the devil. Apparently there were three types of manuscripts prevalent in the Valley of Mexico—histories, legal documents and tribute lists of which there is a single one extant, the Mendoza Codex, at Cambridge University in England. The paper upon which these books were written was made in a long strip and then folded up accordion-wise. The writing ran from left to right and the pages were read from top to bottom just as our books today. Fortunately we know a lot more about the structure of the Aztec ideographs than about the Maya hieroglyphs and it is possible to read almost all the codices we have. Each symbol is composed of a number of word pictures hardly modified through usage. This has led the students to believe that the art of writing was rather new in Mexico at the time of the Conquest.

The names of the towns that appear on the tribute list and in various other codices were written by combining symbols that represent words, the principal syllables of which are found in the town names. For instance, Mazatlan is composed of the symbols for *mazatl* meaning deer and *tlantli* meaning teeth. So we might translate the name of the west coast city as Deer Teeth. However, it is quite probable that such a literal translation should not be made. The suffix *tlan,* derived from the word for teeth, is found in a great many Mexican town names as is the suffix *tepec* which means hill. The sign for Coatepec is composed of the curious pile-like symbol for hill with a snake emerging from its summit, the snake being called *coatl.* Caltepec is "the house on the hill" and it is written with a house symbol on the

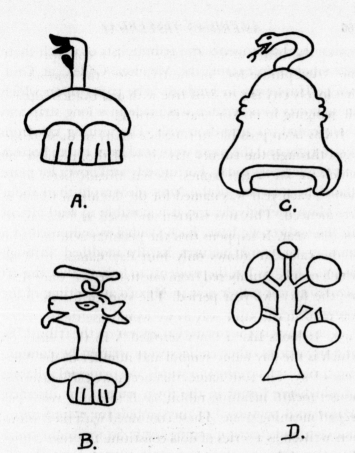

A & B. Mazatlan   C. Coatepec

D. Cuernavaca

NAME GLYPHS OF MEXICAN TOWNS

top of the hill symbol. Cuernavaca is a corruption of the Aztec phrase for "of the tree" and the symbol for that lovely city is a stylized tree with one branch lopped off, hanging in midair near the trunk.

It has been possible to translate many of these name signs through the twenty day signs of the calendar, of which we know the names. As has already been mentioned, each year was named for the day upon which it commenced. This was written and used as a signature for that year. It happens that the peculiar arrangement of the calendar allows only four day names, each of which occurs, numbered from one to thirteen, once during the fifty-two-year period. The symbol for the year was used in the same way as we would use the number 1935. It looks like a fancy scrolled A in the center of which is the day name symbol and number of the New Year's Day. The four names that occur are *calli* meaning house, *tochtli* meaning rabbit, *acatl* meaning reed and *tecpatl* meaning stone. These combined with their numbers written as a series of dots constitute the year name. The rest of the date is written after it, giving merely the day name and number. Aztec number writing differs markedly from that used by the Mayas. The Mayas, as you remember, numbered their days from zero to nineteen, reasoning that no day had elapsed until twenty-four hours had passed. The Aztecs figured them as we do. Their first day was their number one day. Thus they had days running from one to twenty in their month. The units one to nineteen were written usually as dots or circles, one dot or circle for each unit. Occasionally in commercial writings we find a finger being used as a unit in count. It is probable that the dot

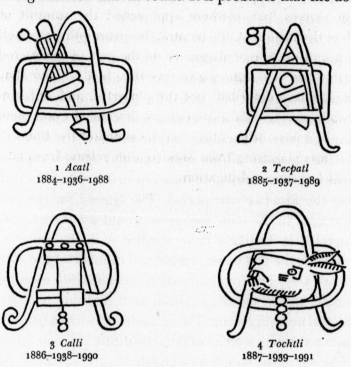

1 *Acatl*
1884–1936–1988

2 *Tecpatl*
1885–1937–1989

3 *Calli*
1886–1938–1990

4 *Tochtli*
1887–1939–1991

TOLTEC-AZTEC YEAR-BEARERS

evolved from the finger nail which is always depicted clearly in these finger counts. Twenty, the beginning of their second order of figures, was represented by a banner; 400 by a stylized feather that looks more like a childish attempt to draw a picture of a pine tree. The symbol for 8000 was a highly ornamented pouch. This occurs rarely. It seems that they seldom needed the fourth order of numbers.

It is quite apparent that at the time of Cortez' arrival the Aztecs had nowhere approached the summit of their development. To be sure, they were going through a minor decline of allegiance on the part of conquered tribes and it is amusing to speculate just how far they might have gone had not the powerful, and unfortunately stifling, European culture descended upon them in the early 16th century. Today much of the finest in the arts is coming from Mexico after release from centuries of cruel subjugation.

CHAPTER SEVEN

CHOROTEGAS AND CHIBCHAS

1

BETWEEN the two areas where architecture was of a permanent type, Mexico and Peru, lies a great area in which archeologists have not been distracted by huge structures and have been able to study more fully the arts and crafts of the former occupants. This area comprises the republics of Central America, and Colombia and Ecuador in South America. A thorough knowledge of this region is extremely important. Through it, it may be possible someday to link the archeological remains in North and South America and arrive at some satisfactory correlation between Maya dates and Peruvian antiquities. We know relatively little of the archeology of Colombia, a little more about Ecuador and a great deal about Central America.

The republics of the narrow, mountainous isthmus connecting North and South America seem to have been the meeting place of migrations from both continents. The mingling of these immigrants with the original people of the region and with each other has made a problem which the ingenuity of the archeologists has thus far failed to solve completely, although the basic lines of the solution have been laid down. According to tradition and to actual material finds, at least three streams of people came down from the north. Two of these followed the west coast and were composed of Nahuatl tribes. The earlier of the two slowly filtered into Central America in the eleventh and twelfth centuries, the later about a hundred years before the conquest by Spain in the early sixteenth century. These people were able to give to Oviedo who was with the Conquistadors a fairly clear picture of their wanderings after they had left Anahuac, the plateau of Mexico. The third group came from the northeast and were Mayas. Their movement probably started with the gradual decline of the Old Empire region and took place before the earlier of the two Mexican invasions along the Pacific. They moved into Honduras and the land east of the Cordillera. From the south the land was invaded by tribes of Chibcha who were probably forced from their old homes by the expansion of the warlike Caribs from Venezuela and the north coast of South America. The original homeland of the Chibcha seems to have been the high plateaus of the Cordillera Oriental from Bogata to Tunja in Colombia.

Just who were the original occupants of Central America is an unsolved problem. Archeological evidence indicates that they were similar in culture to the "Archaic" people of Mexico Valley. They made pottery figurines that are similar to those discussed in Chapter Four and their pottery vessels are also of the same types.

Furthermore, in the great volcanic region of El Salvador, their remains are found buried under as much as forty feet of volcanic ash. Similarly situated sites have been found in Mexico, a fact which indicates a widespread, homogeneous, archaic culture at about the same period in the two regions. However, there are areas in the republic, El Salvador, in which archaic figurines are turned up when the land is plowed. These are closely associated with pottery of the much more highly developed Chorotegas and Mayas. Such finds tell us that the archaic type of art persisted to recent times.

I believe that the linguistic studies that have been made during the last twenty years bear a key to the problem. There are five principal languages spoken by the Indians in the middle of the isthmus: Nahua, Chorotega, Chibcha, Maribio and Tacacho. The tribes speaking Nahua dialects probably represent the latest influx from Mexico, mentioned in a previous paragraph. Those speaking Chorotega dialects, according to some students, are related to people in central and southern Mexico, such as the Otomi and Mazahua, and may represent a people in Mexico earlier than the Nahuatl. The Chibcha are directly connected with the tribes of Colombia. The Maribio dialects have been shown by Lehmann and Sapir to be related to the Hokan family of dialects in southern California and to the Coahuiltecan dialects from Texas and northeastern Mexico. Tacacho has no known relatives.

If we borrow from biology the theory proposed by

students of migration, that the most primitive forms are found on the periphery of a distribution, and if we consider the three tongues, Nahua, Chorotega and Maribio, the following premise seems possible. The earliest expansion, bringing with it the most primitive forms of art, is that widest spread, the Maribio. Similar reasoning would place the Chorotega migration next and the Nahua most recent. So I think we might safely say that the archaic type of work was introduced by Maribio-speaking people and, since they still exist, it is to be expected that even in the most recent deposits archaic wares are to be found. Possibly Tacacho, which Alonso Ponce discovered being spoken at the time of the Conquest in the town of Yacacoyan, a league northwest of Subtiaba on the west coast of Nicaragua, is all that remains of the original tongue and people of Central America.

2

In the northeastern portion of Central America the languages and products of the people are clearly of Maya origin. Probably the best known region, archeologically speaking, is the Uloa Valley in Honduras. Here it seems the Mayas impressed their culture upon an earlier one, the Lenca, which was of Mayence derivation. No magnificent structures are found here but huge mounds remain to be excavated and studied. Tulane University is beginning a campaign in the region and in a decade or two we shall know a great deal about the early history of the area. The pottery that has been recovered, mostly from graves, is pure Maya. It shows to a striking degree the extent to which stylization progressed among these people. Each type of shape is definitely associated with a particular design of decoration. Such slight changes as the addition of a pair of little, nubby handles to a cylindrical vase called for a different decorative pattern. It is possible to completely reconstruct a ceramic piece from a single sherd sufficiently large to give an idea of the decoration.

This region is renowned for its marble vases. These are all cylindrical but they vary in height from true vases to high-rimmed plates. Some of them are equipped with feet of zoömorphic design and all of them are made with handles of animal motif. The sides are decorated with typical Maya god masks in low relief. Although the marble used is generally of poor quality, the workmanship is excellent. These vases are very rare; hardly a score of them are known. That they were highly valued and rare in ancient times is witnessed by the many pottery imitations that are found.

One skull from the region, brought back by the Tulane expedition, is worthy of note. It was found by an Indian on the river bank and brought to Dr. Blom. When he had freed it of the encrusting sand and calcareous cement, he discovered that a jade bead was firmly attached to the palate close to the molar teeth on the right side. Closer examination revealed that three of the upper front teeth had been inlaid. The turquoise is still in place in two of these. Both sets of incisors had been filed in youth to take the "T" shape of the Maya day sign *Ix*. The skull itself shows evidence of deliberate deformation of the usual Maya kind. It is interesting that Bishop Landa, writing in 1564 or earlier, describes such inlay, filing and deformation as being highly regarded by the Maya of Yucatan at the time of the Conquest. He also states that jade beads which were used as money by these people were placed in the mouth of a wealthy dead person to assure him funds in the new world he was entering. This find confirms the statement of the Bishop and his informants. If the entire burial had been found and the period of the interment dated by the mortuary pottery, we might have learned from the discovery how long such practice was used. Dr. Blom suggests that the man had lived during the ninth *bactun,* about 1000 years before the Conquest.

3

The Nicarao tribe of the Chorotega has been described for us by Oviedo. In many respects their social and religious organizations were like those of the tribes found by the Spaniards in Mexico. Doctor Lothrop has published many excerpts from the Spanish historian's account in Chapter II through IV of his monumental work on Costa Rican and Nicaraguan pottery (*Contributions, Heye Foundation Vol. VIII,* 1926, New York). All the buildings of these people were of perishable

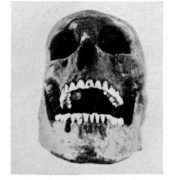

ULOA MARBLE VASE   ULOA SKULL WITH JADE
BEAD
(Courtesy, Tulane University)

MAYA POLYCHROME

PLUMBATE WARE FROM SALVADOR
Found in the Uloa Valley as Trade Goods
(Courtesy, Museum of the American Indian, Heye
Foundation)

materials and similar to the thatched dwellings built today in the region. They clothed themselves in dresses made of cotton and of the beaten bark of trees. The men wore breechcloths and sleeveless tunics beautifully decorated with colored embroidery and woven patterns. The women wore skirts that were knee length for the common people and ankle length for the ladies of high rank. Over the shoulders they wore capes. The men who were warriors wore their hair tonsured in a particular fashion in each tribe. Their bodies were decorated with paints and tattooing. Gold ornaments of Chiriqui manufacture and local jade amulets were suspended on cords around their necks and tied to their arms and thighs. Labrets of gold or bone were worn in the lower lip. The heads were frequently deformed by making a depression along the midline of the skull that "our heads would be better adapted to the burdens we carry."

Among these people agriculture was highly developed. Maize, squash, cotton and cacao were cultivated; tobacco and coca were raised, the former rolled into cigars and the latter chewed with lime to give the effect of the cocaine contained in the leaves. Turkeys, dogs, raccoons and human beings were raised for food. It has been suggested that the excessive human sacrifice and the eating of the bodies of sacrificial victims as a religious act led to this horrible practice of actually raising and fattening humans for consumption as a regular part of the Chorotega diet. Game and fish were and still are abundant in the region so no dietary excuse can be given for the habit.

Of the several arts of these people we have only great quantities of a very fine pottery and some stonework. Grinding stones, or metates, of the most artistic types found in the Americas come from the peninsula of Nicoya and are the product of these people. These are three-legged, thus different from those of similar design made by the Chibchas to the south. Animal motifs supply the design for the best of them. In the illustration the upper one represents a tapir and the lower two, jaguars. Amulets and gorgets of jade and fine stone were made, some of them beautifully decorated with carved design and highly polished. These seem to have replaced the gold work found so abundantly farther south among the Chibchas. War club heads, throwing stick pegs, axes, bark beaters and rubbing stones, meticulously fashioned and polished are found in the graves.

The pottery is pleasing in form and decoration. Dozens of different wares are recognized. These may be divided into three general groups: polychrome, two-color or intermediate, and monochrome wares. As yet little is known of the pottery sequence in the region. Some of the wares, for example the plumbate monochrome, was highly prized as trade goods and examples hailing from a small region in El Salvador are found all over Central America. This ware is a black self-glazing ware that was clearly modeled into effigies. The most abundant and possibly the most interesting ware pro-

TURKEY

PLUMED SERPENT

CRAB

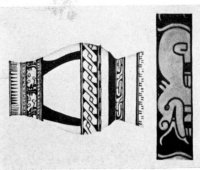

WARRIOR-JAGUAR MOTIF

JAGUAR

MAN

NICOYA POLYCHROME

(Courtesy, Museum of the American Indian, Heye Foundation)

duced is called Nicoya Polychrome. Most of the pieces
of this ware have pear-shaped bodies, though other
forms are found, and are decorated partly in paint and
partly in relief. Many of the specimens bear handles
modeled realistically to represent animal or human
heads. Turkey heads, macaws, other birds, jaguars, mon-
keys, armadillos and man are among the favorites used.
It is interesting to note that the serpent, used so freely
in Mexico and in southern Costa Rica, and the alligator,
which ranks second to the armadillo in Panama, are not
used by the Nicoya Chorotegas. The painted bodies of
the bowls that are not effigies bear decoration that shows
a strong Maya influence. On these such common Maya
motifs as the warrior-jaguar and the plumed serpent
appear frequently. The jaguar alone is another favorite.
The illustration shows the use of these three motifs as
applied by Nicoya artists. Other natural motifs were
employed; some such as the crab and alligator, seem
to have been borrowed from the Chibcha of Panama
and southern Costa Rica.

Tripod wares and whistles, which are found among
Nicoya pottery, are probably derived from South American forms and will be discussed in the following section.
The simple painted wares and monochrome wares are
of widespread derivation extending throughout the pottery areas in the Americas. One or two techniques may
be mentioned here that may have had their origin in
this region. Almost all the polychrome pottery is finished with a varnish of waxes or resins that has pre-

served the beauty to an extraordinary degree. Some of
the incised wares have had the grooves filled with a
white substance that is either infusorial earth or chalk.

The great importance of study of these Nicoya wares
lies in their ancient demand as trade wares, in the use by
the potters of motifs from other regions and in the fact
that Nicaragua seems to have been the meeting place of
North and South American cultures. Thus far the following relationships have been discovered: with the
Maya of the third to seventh centuries * ; with the Maya
of the eleventh and the fifteenth centuries; with the
Toltec Empire at its height in the tenth and eleventh
centuries; and with the Aztec Empire of the fourteenth
to sixteenth centuries.

Stone statues of Chorotega style built into the founda-
tions of Maya Old Empire structures indicate that the
Chorotega antedates the Old Empire. Some of these
statues show stylistic relationship with the Tuxtla statuette which is the earliest dated Maya piece. Chorotega
polychrome wares bear designs borrowed directly from
the Old Empire Maya. Some of these are the plumed
serpent, the jaguar and the profile human head of distinct Maya cast. The presence of Nicoya Polychrome
and of plumbate wares at Copan indicates contact between the Old Empire Maya and the Chorotega. The
connection with the later Maya is more tenuous and

* Morley's correlation is used here as by Lothrop in order to avoid confusion with the published work. The dates should be advanced two and
a half centuries to bring them into keeping with the best correlations as
they are accepted today. See Appendix II.

depends upon certain pot shapes and techniques that may have been derived from the Yucatecan area. The prime example is the chocolate pot, a true Maya invention, a globular pot with slender pouring spout and usually a neck for filling the vessel.

The evidence of the connection with the Toltec and the Aztec Empires is less strong than that with the Old Empire Maya but stronger than that with the later Maya. Certain types of plumed serpent decorations that are more like the representation of that diety in Mexico than in Yucatan and the Peten, and examples of pottery that resemble Cholulu ware done in Nicaragua clay and workmanship, are the strongest links between the Toltec and Chorotega. The Aztec connection is found in the use of the man-jaguar motif—also used in Toltec-Maya regions of Yucatan, as on the decorative panels of the Temple of the Warriors at Chichen Itza—and more definitely in the use of the Earth-Monster of Aztec codices.

To the south the close neighbors of the Chorotega, the Chibcha, had a purely South American culture. There is evidence of some connection between the Chorotega and the Peruvian cultures still farther south but it is in need of much study before we shall be able to link the cultures of the north and those of the south. As yet the three-cornered relationship among the Chibcha, the Chorotega and the Peruvian cultures has not been cleared up.

4

The only area of the Chibcha region that has been studied thoroughly and is free of too much influence from north or south is the Chiriqui region of Panama. The Cauca Valley in Colombia was strongly influenced by Peruvian culture as far north as Pasto. The Costa Rican area was strongly subjected to Nahuatl influence from the Chorotega. Fortunately great quantities of material from the Chiriqui region, exhumed from graves in huge cemeteries or *huacal,* are at Yale University and have been carefully studied. Unfortunately here too no pottery sequence has yet been determined. Since pottery is the key to American archeology the tangle will not be unsnarled until further work is done in Central America.

Along with the pottery, quantities of stone and gold work have been recovered. Unfortunately much of the latter, of which as much as half a million dollars' worth a year for several years was received by an English bank, was consigned to the melting pot. The stone implements consist of arrow points, celts, metates, stools, images and amulets. The arrow and the spear points are usually triangular in crosssection and roughly chipped. Some show signs of pecking, grinding and polishing. The celts are frequently long-necked with swollen heads and are finely polished. The metates range from simple three-legged affairs typical of all Central America to a highly decorated four-legged jaguar type peculiar to the region.

ARMADILLO WARE

FISH WARE

SERPENT WARE   LOST-COLOR WARE   ALLIGATOR WARE

CHIRIQUI TYPES OF POTTERY

CHIRIQUI JAGUAR METATES   NICOYA   ANIMAL ME-
TATES

(After Holmes)

(Courtesy, Dr. G. G. McCurdy & the Connecticut Academy of Arts & Sciences)

The stone stools too vary from simple things to highly ornate affairs. The images carved from stone are rather crude and highly realistic figures of animals, men and women. Jade was used for zoömorphic and phytomorphic amulets but to a less extent than farther north. Among the Chibcha gold was the prime medium for amulets.

About twenty types of pottery are recognized in the Chiriqui region. Of these some were doubtlessly trade wares from the north. Five of them are important enough for discussion in this summary: Armadillo, Serpent, Fish, Lost Color and Alligator wares. Armadillo ware is an unpainted product decorated chiefly with modeled motifs based upon the armadillo. A great variety of shapes were used. The simplest seems to have been derived from the ever present tropical gourd or calabash; other bowls are set upon annular bases or supported by legs. About half of the huge collection of over 4000 pieces at Yale are of this ware.

Although entire armadillos are the predominating motif in the decoration of this yellowish to reddish terra cotta ware, other zoömorphic and human motifs are found and a great many pots are decorated with designs derived from the tail, carapace or head of the armadillo. Curiously only about five percent show any evidence of use. This may have been a purely mortuary ware. Those that have been used are quite greasy and bring to mind Seeman's description of the preparation of a chieftain for burial. The deceased leader was trussed up over a

fire and dried out. To prevent a blaze from the dripping
grease, a bowl was set beneath him to catch it. Unfortunately Seeman did not describe the bowl so that it
might be identified.

A black ware bearing designs incised before the paste
was dry and brought out by filling the incisions with a
white substance is not very frequent in Chiriqui but is
found plentifully a little to the north at Tres Rios,
Costa Rica. This ware differs also from Armadillo in
that it is impervious to water. The design applied is
based upon the serpent. Some of these serpents are
highly realistic while others bear no resemblance at all
to a snake. On this latter kind the design may be traced
back to the zigzag method of depicting realistic serpents.
The puncture patterns represent scales. This serpent
ware shows no influence of Nahuatl design and never
bears a plumed serpent.

Fish ware is so-called because of the predominance of
pieces in which the tripod legs are derived from realistically modeled fish. Some of the examples are painted,
others not. Paint was used more frequently on the inside than on the outside of the bowl. This type of pottery seems to have been one of the principal cooking
wares since most of the examples are well sooted. Apparently the sequence of construction was to model a
"calabash" bowl, apply handles usually of zoömorphic
design, then add a fillet around the rim and lastly add
the legs, which are slit along the back and frequently
contain rattle pellets. This type of tripod ware with

1, Realistic Alligator with Triangular Scales; 2, Alligator with Head Thrown Back and one Front Leg Raised; 3, Simplified Alligator; 4, Much Simplified two-headed Alligator; 5 and 6, "Hieroglyphic" style of representing two-headed and single Alligators

Modified from McCurdy

TWO FIGURINES AND A SQUIRREL WHISTLE FASHIONED IN ALLIGATOR WARE

(Courtesy, Dr. G. G. McCurdy & the Connecticut Academy of Arts & Sciences)

rather long supporting legs is distinctly of South American origin and is not to be confused with the type bearing mammillate legs, found in the Valley of Mexico. The occurrence of these long-legged tripods among Chorotega pottery indicates that the Chorotega and Chibcha were contemporaneous in Central America.

The Lost Color ware is the second largest group in collections. Most of the pieces are bottle-shaped and only a few bear handles. There are, however, a number of shallow tripod bowls known that bear this type of decoration. The paste is yellowish gray and was shaped carefully and polished before being fired. Many if not all of the narrow-necked bottles were modeled in two pieces and welded with clay at the great diameter of the vessel. After the yellow product was fired a design was painted on it with wax; then the entire vessel was coated with a black paint of charcoal, sugar and a resinous substance made from the pods of a legume. When this paint had hardened into a varnish-like film the vessel was placed in hot water that melted off the wax design leaving the negative of it in the original yellow color on a black background. Occasionally an additional color was used by having part of the pot slipped with reddish brown before the wax decoration was applied.

The third largest group of Chibcha ware is Alligator. This is a finely finished pottery with a light cream to yellow slip decorated with black outlines filled with red. It derives its name from the use of the alligator as a decorative motif to the exclusion of all others in the painted work. The shapes are various and include effigies of all sorts. The degree to which the alligator motif has been stylized can be seen better than told. The illustrations tell part of the story. It is in this ware that one of the characteristic trade pieces of the Chibcha is found—whistle figurines. These delightful little objects are to be found all over Central America. I recently saw a beautiful series of them, found in the Uloa Valley of Honduras associated with highly stylized pottery of the Maya Old Empire. The notes produced are three or four in a scale for each whistle. The scale is the same one we use in our music today, not one of the weird scales used by Asiatics or the North America Indians.

To the treasure hunter the gold work found in Chibcha graves has been a lure since the Conquest. It is fascinating. Objects were formed by hammering, casting, repoussé and intricate wire work processes. Most of the hammered work was done in shaping large nuggets. The casts were made by the lost-wax technique. Models were executed in wax or resin and packed into a sand mold. The hot metal melted out the model and the gold solidified in the form. Most of the amulets were modeled after animals, animal-gods and men. I have not seen one instance of a woman's form having been used in Chiriqui gold work. Thinly hammered plaques were used as gorgets. An unmarried woman wore such a plague with a single breast beaten into it in repoussé; a married woman wore a similar gorget with two or more breasts so modeled.

GOLD WORK FROM OAXACA, MEXICO
(Courtesy, Museum of American Indian, Heye Foundation)

Realistic and Conventionalized Alligators

Jaguar-God

Matron's Gorget

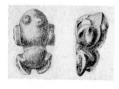

Rare Face Gorget

Resin Model for Gold
Casting

GOLD WORK FROM CHIRIQUI, PANAMA
(Courtesy, Dr. G. G. McCurdy & Connecticut Academy of Arts & Sciences)

The whole artistic character of this gold ware differs from that of the same art as practiced in Mexico as a glance at the illustrations will show. It is of South American derivation and compares better with that used in Peru, to which country we shall now turn.

CHAPTER EIGHT

EARLY PERUVIANS

1

THE opinion among men who should know is that the great Andean civilizations as well as the lesser primitive peoples of the Amazon basin once hailed from Central America. The theory that has been proposed, primarily by the French school of archeologists, that South America was settled by a transoceanic migration from Polynesia seems not to have much support. If such intrepid mariners as the Maoris on their long sea voyages touched upon the South American coast and established colonies there, there is nothing left of them among the peoples that were discovered by the Spaniards. Although the coastal villagers were fisherfolk and resorted to the sea for their livelihood their crafts were by no means developed along the same lines as those of the South Sea Islanders. Everything that has been found in the region points instead to Central America. From the land of the Mayas there are three possible migration routes to South America. One that was followed probably by the antecedents of the coastal civilizations of the Chimu and Nazca was down the west coast all the way. The other routes are down the east coast, one of them

PROBABLE MIGRATION ROUTES FROM CENTRAL AMERICA

following the shore line of South America around to the great rivers, the Orinoco and the Amazon. These water courses were probably travel routes to the interior. It seems to me most probable that the very earliest infiltration into South America followed these for it is only in the low-lying regions of Brazil and the countries to the south that we have found anything that might resemble ancient man. The third route, up the Magdalena, was the one probably followed by the progenitors of the highland civilizations of Tiahuanaco and the later Incas. From the material set forth in the first chapter it would seem that the earliest migrations took place during one of the later glacial periods and that there was a long gap of time before the more highly developed civilizations on the western coast moved in. Dr. P. A. Means places this last migration at about 1000 B. C.

In order to understand more clearly the development of the cultures on the west coast it is necessary for the reader to be aware of the topography. The Pacific coast of Peru is a narrow strip of extremely desert land back of which rises abruptly the western Cordillera of the Andes. The flanks of this high range of mountains are scored deeply with precipitous valleys that support, at least in the bottom land, a tropical forest. The occasional much lower coastal ranges rising sharply from the sea are arid and sterile. Travel between the valleys is so difficult that even today it is necessary to travel either to the sea or to the crest of the main range to go from one valley to the next. Thus in the isolated pockets it is quite probable that there arose small independent groups of people that were self-supporting. The early chroniclers who have preserved for us in some detail

CENTERS FROM WHICH THE PERUVIAN CULTURES SPREAD

the pre-Conquest history of the people as told to them by the Inca historians describe a paternalistic form of government in which the chieftainship was not purely hereditary but was passed, upon the death of the leader, to the most fit member of his family among his sons or brothers. This is curiously parallel with the pre-feudal custom that prevailed in China and may be accounted for as a typically Asiatic trait cropping out among the American Indians who, ages past, were derived from the same stock.

Culturally it seems that the inhabitants of the Andean region were at about the Archaic level when they migrated from their Central American homes. There have been no early Archaic or pre-Archaic evidences found in the region. The earliest civilizations in Peru may be divided into three groups. Two were situated on the coast, they of the Chimu in the north, of the Nazca in the south. The third was confined to the highlands and was destined in time to be the fount from which the powerful empires of Tiahuanaco and of the Incas were to arise and conquer both of the coastal civilizations and extend their power from the Colombian border down into Bolivia.

2

It is apparent that the region now occupied by Trujillo, Peru was the area from which the empire of the Chimu spread. As in the case of the Incas the term Chimu is derived from the Indian's name for their regent, the Chimo, and today the valley is known as the Valle de Chimo. Apparently early in the history the first stage in the expansion was the annexation of the region just to the north, the Valley of the Pacasmayo. From then on their story is one of continual expansion to the north and to the south until they rubbed shoulders with the wild tribes of Ecuador and their highly developed neighbors, the Nazca. It is to this civilization that the great city of Chan-chan just outside modern Trujillo belongs.

Although we have no written history and description of the people dating from their time it has been possible to reconstruct an accurate picture of their life from their pottery, which is decorated with highly realistic paintings and beautifully modeled figures. On the coast nestled among the wind-swept sand dunes, close to the rivers, were small settlements of fisherfolk from whose labors the more inland city dwelling peoples received a considerable portion of their diet. Separating these coastal outposts from the more densely populated verdant valleys was a desert some thirty to fifty miles wide. Stationed on the regular routes across this were sentries or guards to lead the travelers from one place to another.

The boats used by the mariners, as depicted on the pottery from Chan-chan, seem to consist of great bundles of reeds lashed together as rafts with the sides built up. Some of them had a canopied area in the middle and were used probably for transportation rather than for fishing. Another type of boat was made by tying together inflated seal skins. An interesting pot in the National Museum of Archeology of Lima, Peru shows a raft of wood upon which a minor chieftain is seated being towed through the water by three swimmers. All this is evidence that the people were to some degree, at least those on the coast, sea-faring; but among all of it there is nothing that would indicate the highly developed crafts of the Oceanic peoples.

A great variety of fish apparently were caught and used. The maritime scenes on some of the vessels show us men catching by means of lines, hooks and sinkers, skates, spotted shark and dozens of smaller fish. Some of the patterns that have been found indicate what may have been a ceremony to the Sea God. On one pot there are a number of figures bearing animal masks and wearing clothes quite unlike those of the common fishermen more frequently depicted. Possibly they represent the priesthood associated with the sea and fishing. Other decorations tell the story of hunting. Apparently the deer was an important source of meat for the people of the lowland. There are two types of the chase indicated. In one the animals were driven into a netted enclosure and killed by clubs or by a spear wielded with a throwing stick. The other seems to have employed dogs and it is probable that the game was run until exhausted and then killed, in this mode of hunting as in the other.

All the figures depicted are clothed in elaborate costumes consisting of a tunic and skirt bearing decorative designs. It is evident, too, that body painting was exercised to a great extent. The legs, arms and faces of the majority of the figures indicate it. The usual headdress of the men seems to have been a sort of helmet often decorated with a bunch of feathers at the rear and occasionally with some animal head over the forehead. The clothing depicted is sufficient without further

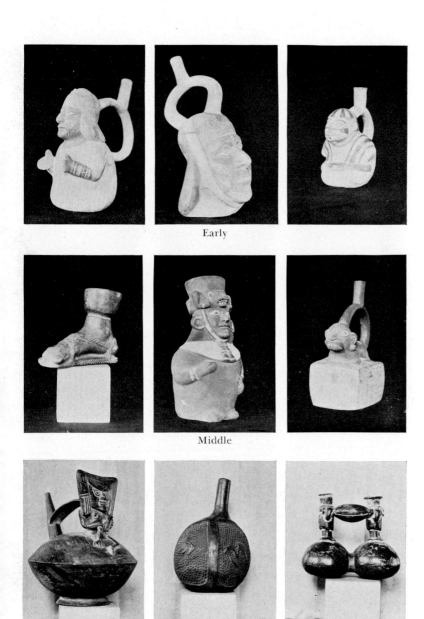

Early

Middle

Late

CHIMU POTTERY
Specimens in the Amer. Mus. Nat. History
Photos. by D. F. Brown

evidence to prove that the people, probably the women, were expert weavers. We have, however, a great deal of direct evidence on this point in scenes showing the growing of cotton and the actual process of weaving. From the latter we see that the loom used in those days, something over 1000 years ago, was in no way different from the one used today by the Indians of the region. It is a modification of the usual primitive hand loom suspended by the upper stick by means of two cords. In a succeeding chapter much space will be devoted to the high art of weaving among the descendants of these early people.

The military dress of the men seems to have been quite like that just described with the addition of a long pad extending down the back from the helmet. The equipment of the warrior is three-fold: spears and spear thrower, a mace-like war club and a broad-bladed hand ax. In addition to using paint, persons frequently adorned themselves with earplugs, necklaces and gorgets. These have been recovered from the cemeteries surrounding the ancient Chimu villages and are made of gold and silver.

Many of the pots bear evidence of a complex religion in which the priesthood wore elaborate costumes of animistic design. Some of them depict highly organized dance rituals; others, gods of various visages. There is one curious pattern that seems to be associated with the warriors, probably in a religious manner; it is a very accurately depicted centipede to the tail of which is attached a bird-masked warrior.

A few pieces of pottery show us buildings. Most of these are represented as being built upon pyramids, some rectangular and others circular. Apparently these people did not approach the Mayas in complexity of decoration or detail of architecture. All the roofs de-

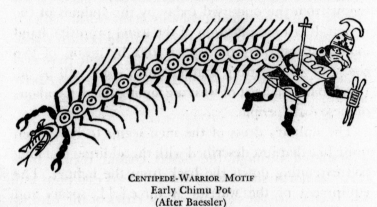

CENTIPEDE-WARRIOR MOTIF
Early Chimu Pot
(After Baessler)

picted show no knowledge of construction other than the simple gabled roof. The buildings seem to have been open on at least one side and many on three. The ornamental roof comb is built here as it was among the Mayas.

From the beautiful portrait vases that have been found it is quite apparent that these people did not practice any of the deformation that is found in the civilizations to the north. The features are fine and of a type indicative of high intelligence and culture. There is no evidence of the slanting Mongoloid eye or cross-eyedness such as is found among the Mayas. The headdress of many of these portrait heads is a skull cap, decorated with geometric or zoömorphic designs, held to the head by a band passing under the chin, and apparently loose over the ears and down the neck. It is among the early Chimu people that we find the most beautiful of all pottery that has ever been made on the American continent and probably in the world, with the exception of the ceramics made during certain dynasties among the Chinese. Certainly no people have ever equaled the Chimu in producing portrait or descriptive wares.

3

Scattered through the desert coastal region from Trujillo north, situated on the few rivers that pour into the Pacific, are the remains of the cities of the Chimu. The most impressive and largest of these are the ruins of Chan-chan. Here are several huge pyramids of debris that probably were terraced and supported temples. These are locally called *huaca,* a name that means merely a place or thing to be reverenced. There has not been a great deal of excavating at Chan-chan or at any of the other ruined cities. Little of the buildings remains. The rapid decay of the adobe structures has been brought about by the occasional rains for several centuries and, since they are close to running water, the modern Indian civilization has utilized the sites for truck gardens and much damage has been done in leveling and in constructing irrigation ditches.

The old city itself covered almost twelve square miles of ground and was surrounded by a high stone wall. The plan resembles that of a modern city with its rectangularly laid out blocks of buildings and squares. The archeologist finds the huge pyramids, some of them approaching two hundred feet in height, irregularly placed. These interfered with an absolutely regular city plan and probably did much to relieve the monotony against the very monotonous background of desert. There were great public gardens and walled and sunken patios developed on rather formal plans. Today the irrigation ditches, quite marked by the deposits of alkaline salts, give us some idea of the geometric outlines of the garden plots. The little digging that has been done has revealed that at the time of occupancy the dull gray walls were covered with white plaster and decorated with colored frescos. At Chan-chan there are two unusually large *huacas* which have been called the Temple to the Sun and the Temple to the Moon, the former being the larger. They are situated to the south of the city across the Rio Moche and probably were surrounded in their pristine glory by numbers of houses and buildings used by the priesthood and their underlings. In the next large valley south of the Moche, that of the Rio Santa, the recent Shipee-Johnson aerial survey discovered a huge Great Wall running for miles inward from the sea and losing itself in the high foothills of the Andes. It runs straight across the rugged terrain until it is lost in the high valleys. In some places

VERTICAL AERIAL PHOTOGRAPH OF CHAN-CHAN

AERIAL VIEW OF TEMPLE AND COURT, CHICAONA
VALLEY

(© Aerial Explorations, Inc.)

it follows the ridges, in others it cut directly across country with no regard for the terrain. Along its course fourteen forts, ranging up to three hundred by two hundred feet in size, have been found. It is believed that this Great Wall was built by the Chimu at the time of the invasion by peoples from the upland. Flanking it are frequently seen well-beaten roads and irrigation ditches. Whether they were used in pre-Spanish times or have developed since then and been forgotten it is impossible to say. However, the desert, particularly in the vicinity of the ruined cities, shows admirable roads leading from one city to another, to the coast and to the mountains; so we may suppose that the roads along the Great Wall itself are ancient and were used for the transportation of troops and supplies.

About fifty miles farther south near the seacoast are several fortified hilltops that are believed to mark the southernmost limits of the empire of Chimu at its greatest expansion in that direction. It has been suggested that the Great Wall and the fragments of short walls discovered by Dr. Olson a few years ago between the Valley of the Santa and Chan-chan were erected largely for defense against invaders. Since the cities on the desert were dependent upon mountain streams for their water supply it was imperative that they draw a line of forts and fortifications far out into the hills to prevent invaders from damming or diverting the rivers and conquering the Chimu in that manner. In fact, Montesinos records that the Incas finally did conquer the Great

Chimu by cutting off his water supply. Many years of patient exploration and excavation must be carried on before we can draw an adequate picture of the great pre-Inca civilizations along the coast of this fascinating country.

From the artifacts that have been discovered and from the legends that were preserved carefully by the Spanish priests, we know that the great Chimu empire fell before the onslaught of pre-Inca people from the highlands and that after some time they again gained independence but never against achieved the high state of art and development of their early days. The pottery of Late Chimu time is far inferior to that which we have just discussed and shows a great deal of outside influence. One of the outstanding changes is the adoption of black pottery, almost to the exclusion of other types. To be sure, about one quarter of the material found is of dark red but among the collections of early material only two or three pieces in every hundred are black. The characteristic stirrup-shaped handle and spout is definitely carried over but the beautifully realistic modeling is lacking. Occasional pieces are found that have a beauty of their own but, in general, the design and the workmanship show decay. Many indications of foreign innovations are found. Geometric designs and highly stylized figures predominate and seem to be derivations, along with a curious double pot linked by means of a bridge, from the early Nazca pottery. This linking of what previously were two clear-cut cultures is probably

THE GREAT WALL AND A FORT
Aerial View
(© Aerial Explorations, Inc.)

due to the conquest of the entire coastal region by the Tiahuanaco, who ante-dated the Incas in the highlands. One curious type of pottery is the whistling pot that seems to have developed extensively in Late Chimu times. It consists of an arrangement of air passages in the neck of the pot, through which the in-coming air rushes and causes a whistling sound as water is poured from the spout. Dr. Means has summed up the characteristics of Late Chimu ceramics succinctly. He says: "The designs, on both the black ware and the red ware, were often of realistic intent, particularly in the modeled part of the ornamentation, but they never achieved the lifelikeness nor the vigor of the best Chimu decorations whether painted or modeled. The explanation of this loss of skill, for such it seems to have been, lies perhaps in the cloying and conventionalizing influence of Tia-huanaco II art, so long paramount on the coast."

Fortunately we have preserved for us several beautiful pieces of textiles from the Late Chimu period. On the pottery of the early period we have seen that the rich and diverse clothing has been depicted. From the ornaments of the late period we can get some idea of the workmanship. Two materials were employed on the loom—cotton and wool. The most important of the several types of Peruvian cotton is what is today known as Peruvian Full or Moderately Rough. This type of cotton is a perennial, growing to a height of about fifteen feet. The fibers are long and equipped with tiny hook-like projections that make it possible to spin extremely thin threads. Some of the finest textiles are woven with twice as many threads to the inch as are used today with the aid of machines. The wool used for making the woolen thread was that of vicuña. Here, again, the ancient spinners and weavers often caught twice as many threads of weft to the inch as we do with the same wool and with machine spinning. The thread itself was spun with the usual primitive spindle shaft and whorl. Even today it is possible to see in the upland country natives going about their business, twirling a spindle and making thread. The looms used have been described. They were seldom wider than two feet although one or two have been found with a spread greater than four feet. Smaller looms for the manufacture of girdles, fillets and slings are known, even to one only one-half inch wide. Some of the cottons were left in their natural colors. The old Spanish chroniclers tell us that cotton was naturally grown in white, shades of brown and yellow and even several in pale blue. In addition to using natural colors, the ancient weavers resorted to dyeing. Unfortunately very little study has been expended upon the methods and materials used for this by the Peruvians. Dr. Valette analyzed several samples and found that calcium silicate, aluminum silicate and iron oxide were all used as mordants in ancient Peru. Cochineal, a substance derived from a tiny insect that lives on cactus, and indigo, a plant dye, have been identified as two of the coloring materials used. What the others were we do not know.

LATE CHIMU TAPESTRY
(Courtesy, Mus. of Fine Arts, Boston, Mass.)

PELICAN MOTIF TEXTILE PIECE NO. 23
Mus. of Fine Arts, Boston
Double-faced Cloth—Late Chimu 1100–1400 A. D.

Many types of weaving were employed; plain webs of ordinary weave, double-faced cloth, gauzes and voiles, net work, featherwork and tapestries predominate. There were probably never better craftsmen than these early Peruvians in the art of tapestry. Much of their work exceeds in beauty and workmanship that of the Middle Ages in Europe and modern workers in the art have adopted more than one Peruvian technique in improving the product of today. Very frequently the pieces of tapestry were of a coarse cotton base decorated with the colored wool. It is impossible for me at this time to go into full detail of their textile art. However, the pieces figured will give the reader some idea of the ancient craftsman's ability. It must be borne in mind that the pieces we have have survived the ravages of time for at least five hundred and, in many cases, almost a thousand years.

4

At the time of the Early Chimu dynasties in northern Peru there reigned in southern Peru, namely in the vicinity of Ica and in the country north and south, the Nazca civilization. We owe to Dr. Uhle most of our knowledge of this early culture as, as a matter of fact, we owe most of our knowledge of coastal Peru. Whereas Chimu art is noted for its realism, that of the early Nazca is symbolical and, although there are many early realistic pieces, the majority are decorated with designs that are highly conventionalized men and animals. One

PART OF A TAPESTRY BORDER

PERUVIAN TAPESTRY, LATE CHIMU
(Courtesy, Museum of Fine Arts, Boston)

of the dominating animal figures found on early pots
has been called the Spotted Cat. This curious beast is
usually serpentine in shape with a full view presentation of the face and a side view of the body with the tail
whipped back over the arched rump. The name is derived from the blotches that decorate the flanks. The

SPOTTED CAT-DEMON
(After Seler)
Early Nazca Pot
Ethnological Mus., Munich

face is curious and in many instances almost ludicrous.
The semi-diamond-shaped eyes are frequently joined
together with lines that make the beast look bespecta-
cled. The whiskers are so highly conventionalized that
at first glance it seems as though the beast were holding
its chin in its hands, and all I have seen have a protruding tongue. This design is probably a representation of
some deity.

A development from it is probably the cat demon in
which this curious cat's face is superimposed upon a
human body which is appareled in a dress extending
below the knees, that is often bordered with realistic or

highly conventionalized heads. Often the outspread arms are shown grasping severed heads by the hair. Other times a large curved knife or club is found in one hand and a grisly head in the other. Sometimes this cat demon is equipped with wings and from this form it is only a slight step to the highly conventionalized so-called bird demons.

I must not let you draw the conclusion that all early Nazca decoration is of demons and wild beasts. There

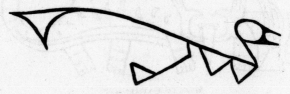

HIGHLY CONVENTIONALIZED BIRD DESIGN
Late Nazca Pot
Ethnol. Mus., Berlin

is a plentiful supply of pots from this period that are rather conventionalized portrait pots. Usually only the head is modeled and the belly of the pot forms the obese torso of some dignitary. Even in these the degree of realism in the modeled and painted decoration is slight, most of the pots being highly conventionalized. In every collection of early Nazca pottery and less frequently in Early Chimu there are specimens, vividly portraying the acts of reproduction, which may have been used in fertility and agricultural rites. These portrayals are so realistic that it is impossible to figure specimens.

As I have already indicated in the case of the Chimu,

Early

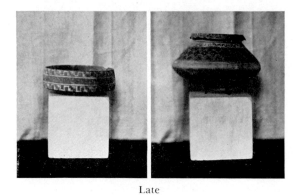

Late

NAZCA POTTERY

Specimens in Amer. Mus. Nat. History

Photos. by D. F. Brown

the period following the Tiahuanaco invasion brought about a general fusion of the coast cultures. So, in many respects, the late Nazca artifacts resemble those of the Late Chimu. However, I must point out here that the change was one not so much of Nazca style as of Chimu style for even before the conquest the more southern people were practicing an art that was highly conventionalized.

5

While the Chimu and Nazca people were developing their highly artistic culture on the lowlands, the people who lived in the mountainous regions of the Andes were slowly evolving from the Archaic stage to a strongly characterized civilization. To this early upland culture the name Tiahuanaco has been given because at the place of that name on Lake Titicaca the first extensive study of it was made. This early upland culture extended in some form or other the whole length of the Andes from Ecuador to Bolivia. During its later stages it reached its height in the *puno* of Peru. While the Chimu and Nazca had to be satisfied with buildings of adobe and idols modeled in clay, the people living in the high valleys made their buildings and idols of stone. The civilization has been divided into two culture periods that are numbered one and two. Of the first we know very little and it is characterized chiefly by the type of architecteure which employed the use of gigantic stones, many of them weighing over one hundred tons. These were shaped and fitted into position to form buildings and battlements high on the walls of the mountainous valleys.

It is quite probable that the early Tiahuanacoans carried on extensive trade with the coast people. Each had important contributions to make to the other. In the highlands copper, silver and gold could be mined. The vicuña that supplied the wool for the coastal weavers is found only in the high country. These are things that we know the lowland people used and must have obtained from their highland neighbors. On the other hand, the coast supplied the uplanders with many things that they lacked—cotton, many sorts of vegetables and fruits. In later years, when the land was all under the reign of the Incas, the coastal peoples shipped sea foods into the mountains and it is possible that the same thing occurred in the earlier times. Probably the most important contribution of the coast to the mountain country was the appreciation of design in both weaving and pottery.

It is of the second culture that we have some information. The people continued their megalithic building but the workmanship is of a far higher order. The wall surfaces are smoother and the joints between the carved blocks more cleanly cut. The art of these people is represented by a wealth of carved stonework. At some of the old ruins the walls are decorated with a great many geometric designs. At others the decoration consists of highly conventionalized god figures and priest figures.

Early   Classic

Decadent

Coastal

TIAHUANACO POTTERY
Specimens in Amer. Mus. Nat. History
Photos. by D. F. Brown

Many of these are zoömorphic. The pottery that has been found is a painted ware employing the same designs as are found in the stone carving. There is really very little metal work considering the amount of it in the succeeding culture. However, there is a sufficient amount of it scattered throughout the area occupied to lead us to believe that the Tiahuanaco craftsmen were capable in this line as well as in the other arts. Nowhere in the region is found any work that even closely approximates the beautiful realistic work of the early Chimus. In general, Tiahuanaco art is closely allied to that of the Nazca people, the design usually being highly stylized or geometric.

As among the Nazca the Spotted Cat was a dominant motif, so among the Tiahuanaco the puma predominates as a source of decoration. Considerable excavation has been carried on at a city to the north, Chavin, as well as at the type locality, Tiahuanaco. Here the material found represents a much higher degree of development and probably much later than that on the shores of Titicaca. The carving is extremely ornate and shows all the evidences of artistic decadence. Still farther north, in Ecuador, at this same time there were developing a series of cities that have been only touched as far as study and excavation is concerned. Dr. Saville has worked along the coast and to some extent into the upland country. The material that has been turned up is related for the most part very closely to Tiahuanaco in style and execution. It is quite probable that further work both in the north and to the south of the Peruvian-Bolivian highlands will show a greater extension of the Peruvian cultures than we are now aware of.

Some time early in the history of the upland culture of Peru a series of great leaders arose with the power to extend the empire. We know definitely that it was they who invaded the coastal regions and brought to a close the early Chimu and early Nazca periods. From each of these cultures the upland people derived something and to each of the lowland groups they contributed at least a veneer that existed for some time. However, in time the rugged mountaineers lost their power on the coastal regions and the two former civilizations there recovered, and developed their late stages that have been described in previous pages. Whether the north and southward extensions occurred at the time of this coastal invasion or whether they occurred at a later time and thus drew the forces of the Tiahuanaco leaders away from the coast and allowed the Chimu and Nazca dynasties to reign again we do not know. The history of the land as handed down to us by the Spanish from the native historians is too confused to be unraveled at present. Further excavation extending from northern Chile to southern Colombia must be undertaken and completed before we have anything like a unified picture of the pre-Incaic history of the land as shown by its archeology.

Recapitulating the story of the Andes as far as we have gone, we find that from about the beginning of the

Christian era until around 500 A. D. there developed along the coast of Peru and probably Ecuador many small unified groups of people that were later fused into the Nazca at the south, the Chimu in northern Peru and the Tuncahuan in Ecuador. These were civilizations noted for their architecture in adobe, their superb ceramic and textile arts and highly developed agriculture. At the same time in the high inter-Andean plateaus the early Tiahuanaco culture noted for its architecture in stone and sculpture was slowly building up. At the close of this period there seems to have been about a century of contact and conflict between the coastal and mountain folks, the outcome of which was victory for the more hardy highlanders. Then followed a period of about three hundred years during which the lowland and highland cultures were fused and many characteristics exchanged, to the decided advantage of the Tiahuanacos. Some time about the close of the first Christian millennium the overlordship of the up-landers began to disintegrate and soon each valley again held an individual group of people developing along its own lines. For the next three hundred years the coastal societies again began to amalgamate in the same groups as before their conquest but their civilizations showed strongly the conventionalizing mark of their former conquerors.

CHAPTER NINE

THE INCAS

1

DURING the period of decline that led to the elimination of the Tiahuanaco culture there developed among the many small tribes of the highlands one whose leadership was soon to dominate almost the entire west coast of South America. Somewhere between Cuzco and Lake Titicaca lie the original lands held by the Incas. When they had developed to a great power there were many legends dealing with their phenomenal rise. These, in general, can be divided into two classes—a highly ornamented group that was prepared and perpetuated for the consumption of the working people and another much more likely group, filled with chicanery and cleverness, that was told among the rulers themselves. A third story of their origins is now being put together by the archeologists. The legend that probably was told most frequently to the common people was that the Incas were descendants of the Sun and that in the early times they issued forth from the Mountain of the Three Windows to lead their people in the conquest of the Andean area. The same tale told more truthfully among the leaders themselves tells of an

ambitious mother who secretly clothed her son in a
garment bespangled with tiny golden plates and, upon
a market day, had him step forth in the early morning
sun from a window above the trading populace and

THE INCAIC EMPIRE: SOLID BLACK AT ITS INCEPTION.
SHADED AT ITS GREATEST EXTENT

proclaim himself son of the Sun and their ordained
leader. His glittering clothing and authoritative mien
led these humble folks to build up the story that was
passed down among them from generation to generation. Those students who have applied themselves to
the dozen or so variations of these two basic myths have
built up a story that seems to satisfy the case. We now

believe that this powerful group of leaders sprang from a family of lower chieftains who were ambitious to rule the former empire of Tiahuanaco and gained their ends through trickery and guile. The leadership of the Incas was not a very long one before the Spaniards came into Peru. They had extended their power to the north and to the south through the mountains, to the sea on the west and into the Amazon jungle on the east. The story of the reign of each of the leaders from about 1100 onward has been given to us by the Spanish chroniclers who had it from the Court historians. Probably the most authoritative of these old accounts is that of Garcilasco de la Vega who himself was of Inca blood.

The first of these leaders who seems to be more than a mythical figure is Sinchi Roca. His name tells us that he was one of the war chieftains of which each small community had one. During the early beginnings of the Inca dynasty these *sinchi* were chosen by the heads of the households in each community to lead them in warfare and, at the termination of the project, became again merely the heads of households. Apparently this war leader, Roca, succeeded in making himself a permanent leader and founded the dynasty of his tribe. He held sway from about 1105 to 1140 and dominated the immediate region of Cuzco and the land to the south. It is doubtful if he held any control outside of the Urubamba Valley.

The ruins on the pass to the south that are pointed out as the out-posts of his domain are of a type of ma-

sonry that leads us to believe that they were built long
before the rise of Sinchi Roca. They are of the crude
pirca masonry of the early Tiahuanaco culture. There is
considerable doubt as to who exactly was his queen or
Coya. In later days it was customary for the Inca to
marry his sister for his chief wife and to take the
daughters of allied chieftains to make up his harem. Although some of the chroniclers relate that Sinchi Roca
had as his *Coya* his own sister, others have him married
to the daughters of various neighboring chieftains. It
seems much more probable that the former is true since
a wise man, and he certainly seems to have been one,
setting out to found a dynasty would be much more
likely to have his sister as first wife and to marry the
daughters of neighboring powerful chieftains as second-
ary wives with equal rank, thus avoiding antagonism.
Upon the death of this the historically first Inca, Lloque
Yupanqui, his son, became ruler and extended the
power of the dynasty to the Titicaca basin and along the
western shore of the lake. In addition to these barren
uplands, he left to the coming Incas a custom that probably accounted for the future great power. His first official act after the period of mourning for his father's
passing was to make a trip of inspection to all parts of
his kingdom. In that way he came to know personally
the local leaders throughout the area under his control
and to meet with the various chiefs who were his neighbors, many of whom voluntarily became his vassals.

The third Inca, Mayta Capac, ruled from about 1195

to 1230. It was this leader who discovered the ruins of Tiahuanaco on Lake Titicaca and from then on Inca architecture developed in strides and followed the lines of that monumental city. Mayta Capac extended the Inca power as far south as La Paz, Bolivia. When his conquests to the south had been amalgamated entirely with the empire, he turned his attentions to the sea on the west. After that the upper portions of all the river systems in southern Peru were under his control. His contribution, in addition to land, is said to be the famous Inca vine bridges which astounded the Spaniards when they conquered the country. About 1230 the reign passed to Capac Yupanqui, the fourth Inca. It was during his period of leadership that the powerful coastland chiefs were conquered and made vassals to the Inca. His great contribution was that of transferring entire villages of the conquered people to districts already completely under the sway of the dynasty and at the same time sending entire communities made up of people who were completely under his sway to the newly conquered region. In making these exchanges of colonies considerable forethought was used in transferring groups of people back and forth to localities that were as nearly like their original homes as possible. Thus the error of attempting to colonize the low, hot coastal belt with emigrants from the high, cold mountain pleateaus was never made. At the close of the Inca Capac Yupanqui's reign the empire was considerably larger than that held by Sinchi Roca. It now exceeded the area of all of New England and New York. Such an extensive country varying from arid coastal deserts to the barren *puno* necessitated a considerable government machinery to keep it functioning properly. Government garrisons were established at strategic places; roads, temples, store houses and the like were built where they would do the most good in keeping consolidated the various tribes under the central authority of the Inca at Cuzco. By the time of the accession of Inca Roca in 1250, the hereditary leaders were highly trained in the routine of government during their youth and it was always uppermost that they extend the beneficent reign of their family. The Inca Roca ascended to the throne at the beginning of a very critical time in the expansion of his empire. Until now the people conquered were more or less of the same stock. It was this man's duty to invade the area to the southeast held by an ethnologically distinct group. The wars that were waged to conquer the Chanca lasted through the rules of three Incas and were not settled until almost a century had passed.

Inca Roca ruled until about 1315. He was followed by the only Inca leader who was not warlike, Yahuar Huaccac. During the thirty-two years of his reign little or no area was added to the empire. Two small regions in the northern part of the Chilean desert were conquered by his brother in the early part of his reign. His son and successor, Hatun Tupac, rose to leadership in 1347 and ruled until 1400. Fortunately he was a

much more powerful man than his father and a great
warrior, for hardly had he come to manhood when the
Chanca confederacy openly rebelled against the Inca
dynasty. It is related that during the early stages of this
rebellion the young prince, who had been exiled from
Court because of his contempt for his father, was visited
by the spirit of Viracocha, the Creator-God, from whom
mythologically the Inca line had sprung. The message
from the deity to the young man was that he command
his father in the name of Viracocha to build up the defenses of the realm and turn back the invaders. This the
prince promptly did with himself as the leader of the
army. When he returned victorious he turned to his
weak father and without mincing words told him that
he had betrayed his trust as leader and could no longer
consider himself as the ruler of the empire but that he,
his son, was now the Inca. With his coronation, he
changed his name to Inca Viracocha. During his rule
he extended the Inca power as far south as Tucuman in
northwestern Argentina. He also brought under the
sway of his scepter several provinces to the northwest of
Cuzco and started the Inca expansion in that direction.
In addition to being a great and powerful warrior Inca
Viracocha was greatly interested in the welfare and com-
fort of his people. It might be said, however, that most
of his improvements, and especially those in areas recently conquered, were done with an eye toward building up a feeling of good will toward the conquerors.
He built extensive irrigation systems, great causeways

and roads and extended the efficient system of food storage that was common within the thoroughly Incaized areas to the very frontiers of the newly conquered land.

It took the next Inca, Pachacutec, three years to make his tour of inspection of the domain left him in 1400 by Viracocha but even so he was unable to visit personally every settlement in his country as had his ancestors. With so large a country he realized that it was important that he have thoroughly reliable rulers scattered through the country to assist him. For these tasks he selected his brothers. This allowed him to divide his time between the problems of government and the expansion of the empire and relieved him of much of the detail that had fallen previously upon the shoulders of the Inca. It was during the reign of Pachacutec that the great northward expansion took place. It was he that conquered the coastal regions as far north as the land of the Chimu. Under his aegis the educational and religious systems of the country were thoroughly revamped. He is credited with being something of a philosopher and moralist. Garcilasco has recorded many of his sayings such as: "He that reviles another, injures himself"; "The noble and famous man is known by the patience he shows in adversity"; "Drunken-ness, anger and madness go together; but the first two are voluntary and to be removed whereas the last is perpetual." This great man died in 1448 and left his kingdom to his son, Tupac Upanqui, who was a worthy follower of his father.

During his reign the wild lowland tribes to the southeast were brought under the partial control of the Inca. This was done more to consolidate the true eastern borderlands of the empire than to extend the imperial control. To the north the power of the dynasty was extended to what now constitutes the Ecuador-Colombia border. To the south conquests were made far down into Chile so that at the close of his rule in 1482 the Inca controlled almost two-thirds of the western part of South America. It was during the reign of this Inca that an amazing expedition set out to explore the Pacific Ocean for islands reputed to lie far to the west of Ecuador. Some of the early Spanish historians identify these islands with the Galapagos Archipelago. Whether these were the islands visited and brought under the Inca sway it is impossible to say. Thus far there have been no discoveries among the islands that would lead to the belief that they were visited and conquered by this great group of South American people. However, the legend is there and it remains for future archeologist-explorers to discover just which group of islands of the several lying off the west coast of the continent are those mentioned in the story. When the old man was dying he called to him his next of kin and those of the nobility who were available and before them and with their agreement appointed his son, Titu Cusi Hualpa, as his successor. He ruled as Inca Huayna Capac from 1482 to 1529.

It took him many years to make the required tour of

inspection of his now enormous empire. As a matter of fact, the land controlled was so large that only a man of great wisdom and tremendous personal power could possibly hope to hold it together. During his reign there arose the first internal rebellion. His half-brother, Capac Huari, attempted with the aid of his mother to wrest the rule from the young Inca. The uprising of Huayna Capac's half-brother at the beginning of the reign was really the beginning of the decline of the Inca dynasty. The advent of the Spaniards in 1530 brought about the final disintegration. The last true Inca died in 1529.

2

During the early periods of the Inca dynasty the architecture of the people was not highly developed. The stone walls of the buildings and fortifications were composed of what is called *pirca* masonry. This is quite distinctive and is made by laying up dry rather rough stones with no sharply marked courses and with no particular care to the finish of the surface. The structures built after the reign of Mayta Capac, who discovered the ruins of Tiahuanaco, show the marked influence of that more ancient civilization upon the architecture of the Incas. From that time on, more and more of the walls were formed from cut stones carefully laid and fitted together. There are hundreds, probably thousands, of Inca ruins scattered from one end of the central Andean area to the other. Some of them, as those in Cuzco, were used by the Spaniards as the basis for the governmental and ecclesiastical buildings that they erected after the Conquest. Today many of the most lasting buildings and those best built have walls that were laid during Inca times.

Farther to the north lie the famous ruins of Macchu Picchu. This great city perched high on a crag above a torrential mountain stream was explored thoroughly and excavated by Dr. Bingham of Yale. It consists of several large buildings and plazas supported by retaining walls and protected by outlying defenses situated about two thousand feet above the river valley. Today it is probably as difficult to approach as in the time of the Incas. The people who lived there supported themselves by crops grown on beautiful terraced hillsides and by herds of llama and vicuña that grazed on the flat, barren mountain tops nearby. Wherever one goes in the rugged country flanking the high Andes are visible the extensive terraced lands of the Incas. This terracing was absolutely necessary for an agricultural people living in such wild and desolate country. It was only by means of it that enough level ground could be held in place against the torrential rains for raising the necessary food for the cities. Today the little towns, snuggled deep in the valleys or hanging high on the hillsides, depend upon these ancient areas and similar, more modern ones for their sustenance. Great irrigation systems wend their ways up the steep flanks of the canyons to bring the necessary water from high in the mountains to the

MACCHU PICCHU

COLCA VALLEY TOWN OF
LLANCA, LOWER LEFT CENTER,
AGRICULTURAL TERRACES

MACCHU PICCHU

AMPHITHEATER, MARAS PAMPAS

(© Aerial Explorations, Inc.)

arable land. It is probable that the great concentration of the population during Inca times was in such easily defended mountain crag cities as Macchu Picchu. When the Spaniards disrupted the empire and the cities fell into decay it was only the hardier and probably the less intellectual groups that could survive life on the high, barren *puno* where the residents must depend upon their flocks and a sparse crop of potatoes for their diet.

The mountain cities of the Incas in the time of the empire were connected by well laid out roads crossing the high Andes, along which were stationed at regular intervals rest houses, barracks and store houses. These were of high necessity to the unity of the domain. Along these roads couriers were constantly passing, bringing news of victories and reports from outlying settlements of the capital of the nation, Cuzco. Along them the Inca led his troops. Along them great caravans carrying the produce of the lands traveled. They were the arteries of the nation and, unfortunately, they played a great part in its downfall for they allowed the Spanish troops easy passage from one area to another. Gutierrez de Santa Clara who saw them soon after the Conquest claimed that these Inca highways surpassed those of the Romans. Bridges were built from canyon wall to canyon wall across the swift rivers by means of fiber ropes, some almost a foot in diameter. These were fastened securely into massive masonry piers. Across the rope cables thus formed sticks were lashed firmly and covered with a coarse matting. Additional ropes flung across formed a sort of handrail. Such swaying bridges were not uncommon and today when they are missing it is necessary to make detours not infrequently occupying days of time to cross a river less than one hundred feet wide. Swamps were bridged with excellently built causeways and in at least one case a pontoon bridge comprised of large rafts made from bundles of reeds was used to carry a highway across a lake.

The system of couriers was remarkable. Dr. Means has culled several records from the Chronicles, that I repeat here. The return trip from Quito in northern Ecuador to Cuzco in southern Peru was made in twenty days, a feat that cannot be approached in these modern days except by airplane. From Lima to Cuzco the time given is three days and I doubt that it can be equaled today. At present a traveler would take about fifteen days using railroad and steamer to travel one way between the first two points; between Cuzco and Lima, more nearly a week than the three days of the Inca runners. The distance between the first two points is about twelve hundred miles. By walking constantly at a pace of about five miles an hour it would thus take about two hundred and forty hours or ten days. When we remember that a message was carried not by one man but by hundreds, each doing his stint between courier stations, and when we consider that the runners had such a perfect system of highways, it is not so wonderful a feat as modern travel in the tropics would lead us to believe.

Many of the modern villages and towns scattered through the mountain region have incorporated in their name the word *tambo* or *tampu*. This is the name given to the Inca rest houses that lined the highways. In general they are stone buildings with hard-beaten dirt floors divided into several rooms the walls of which were neatly plastered. Sometimes they were so built that the rooms were in a straight line. Others were U-shaped forming the sides of a court. In the immediate vicinity there was usually a well-built store house and an adequate water supply. Today the explorer of the high Andes frequently finds rest and protection from the cold winds sweeping down from the snowy mountains against the ruined walls of an old rest house.

3

It almost seems to be a rule in the Americas that when a people developed the art of architecture to a high degree we know very little about their minor arts. This may be because archeologists have paid more attention to design and decoration of buildings when such are present and less attention to the smaller works of art. This is true of the civilizations in Middle Mexico, in Yucatan and in the high Andes. Among the less durable remains of the early Peruvian civilizations searchers, particularly Dr. Uhle, have accumulated a wealth of material of high artistic value in the form of pottery and some metal work.

During Incaic times we know that the people must have made a great many portable things of beauty. Those that have been recovered and studied are relatively few considering the great extent of the Inca empire. The pottery that has been found seems to be entirely a utilitarian ware. The vessels have shapes that suit them to household duties. There are bowls, vases, water bottles, colanders, dippers and other shapes that indicate their use. Probably the most characteristic of all the Inca pottery is the aryballus, a slender-necked water bottle which was carried on the back. Low down on each side of this type of pot are a pair of ears through which a carrying rope was passed and looped up onto a small projection at the base of the neck of the flask.

The Inca design is for the most part purely geometric and it is on these aryballi that we see it in its purest and best style. A great many of these water bottles have the design on one face only, that which would be exposed to view when the flask is being carried on the back. Some of them, particularly those of the later periods, have designs based upon some natural motif either plant or animal. On these the decoration frequently is continuous about the body of the ware. It is greatly to be desired that further study of the scattered Incaic pieces of pottery be carried on. There is a considerable quantity of it, all told, known to us but most institutions have only a few pieces and a complete study will require extensive travel on the part of the student.

The metal work of Inca times is exquisite. The same

THIN GOLD CUPS
University of Pennsylvania Museum
(Courtesy, Museum of Modern Art)

can be said about this as about the pottery. There is much of it known but it is well scattered through the museums and collections of the world. Unfortunately the metals used were primarily gold and silver and the Spanish conquistadors, having no care for their loot except as bullion, melted down for the gold value pieces of art that can never be replaced. Gold and silver were used by the Incas not because they were valuable metals but because they were easily worked metals and the result was that the Spaniards found hoarded together tons of these substances so precious to the European world. The Incas gladly gave it to their conquerors to ransom their last leader, Atahualpa, whom the Spaniards conveniently murdered after his ransom had been paid. The pieces of metal work now in existence have come from two sources. Archeologists have excavated some from the ruins. Others have been found in the burial grounds opened up during road building and by the torrential rains. A good deal recovered by the latter method unfortunately was consigned to the melting pot. Today Peru has remedied that to some extent by paying a little more than its worth in gold for the original piece. Many of the smaller objects represent animals. These were probably the gifts presented by the local chieftains in the Temple of the Sun during the ceremonies that opened the Incaic year. Upon first examination one is struck by the similarity in the sculpture in metal of today's craftsmen. The little silver alpaca from the collections of the American Museum of Natural

History is an excellent example of the careful and thoughtful type of work produced under the Incas.

Probably the most thoroughly studied of the handicraft productions are the textiles. These are a development of similar fabrics produced during the late Tiahuanaco, Chimu and Nazca periods. Most of the Incaic textiles are tapestries and brocades. The designs, beautifully executed in many colors, are most frequently geometric, thus differing from the material of the earlier period, on which conventionalized animal forms are the principal decoration. Many of the beautiful tapestries have come down to us in the form of mummy wrappings. The dignitaries of the Incaic rule were all carefully mummified and wrapped in yards and yards of fine fabric. Over this a beautifully decorated final shroud was placed, upon which frequently was painted the human features. These mummies were venerated greatly and were brought out to take part in many of the ceremonies associated with the state religion, Sun Worship. At Cuzco the mummies of all the Incas were kept in the Temple of the Sun and presided at the altar during the pageantry that ushered in the new year.

Other phases of the artistic ability of people, which are seldom preserved for an extinct civilization, are music and literature. Fortunately, these were chronicled by several of the Spanish priests at the time of the Conquest. The literature may be divided into two classes—drama and poetry. Much of the drama was closely woven into the ceremonies that occupied so many hours

Aryballi

INCA POTTERY
Specimens in Amer. Mus. Nat. Hist.
Photos. by D. F. Brown

of the aristocratic classes. However, there seems to have
been also a group of plays erected about more homely
themes and used in the smaller villages by the common
folk. The poetry is some of the best that has been produced under the conditions of early civilizations. Dr.
Means has translated from the original Quechua several
poems which have been quoted in the accounts of the
early Spaniards in Peru. There is just room here to re-
quote two of them, both from Garcilasco's manuscript.
Dr. Means has made no attempt to write a poetic version
but has merely translated them.

> "Beautiful princess,
> Thy dear brother,
> Thy cup
> Is now breaking.
> So for this,
> There is thunder,
> Lightening;
> Thunder bolts falling.
> But, princess,
> Thy water,
> Dropping rains
> Where sometimes also
> There will be hail,
> There will be snow.
> The maker of the earth,
> Pachacamac Viracocha
> For this duty
> Has blessed thee,
> Has created thee."

A simple love song runs:

"To this my song,
Thou shalt sleep,
In the dead of night
I shall come."

The following prayer addressed to the Creator-God
and translated by Dr. Means is one of many that fortified the belief of the early padres that the Apostle St.
Thomas in his journeyings had reached the New World
and attempted to establish Christianity.

"Oh Pachacamac!
Thou who has existed from the beginning,
Thou who shall exist until the end,
Powerful but merciful,
Who dids't create men by saying,
'Let Man be,'
Who defendest us from evil,
And preserveth our life and our health,
Art thou in the sky or upon the earth?
In the clouds or in the deeps?
Hear the voice of him who implores Thee,
Grant him his petitions,
Give us life everlasting,
Preserve us and accept this our sacrifice."

That surgery and the medical arts were practiced by
these early people we have ample evidence. Many skulls
have been found that show the signs of successful trepanning. It was used probably as a remedy for head-
aches and possibly insanity, the hole being cut into the
skull in order to let out the evil spirit.

That these ancient surgeons were guided by purely

SILVER ALPACA
(Courtesy, Amer. Mus. Nat. Hist.)

SILVER LLAMA
(Courtesy, Amer. Mus. Nat. Hist.)

medical or therapeutic ideas in performing this opera-
tion is extremely doubtful. It was probably used as a
form of magic. I suspect that much of our modern medi-
cine was first practiced with this end in view. Dr. Mc-
Gee has offered an interesting study of trepanning in
which he sets forth the idea that the art is a derivative
of head-hunting! His explanation is that when actual
decapitation for purposes of magic went out of style the
practice of cutting out a small piece of the skull was
substituted. This fragment carried with it all the charm
value of a complete skull and the victim was left living,
possibly as a slave. Whether the Incas had advanced to
the stage of medical knowledge calling for trepanning
or whether they practiced it from a purely magic point
of view I do not know. We may find the answer in the
future—and then again we may not. We do know that
they had a fairly well developed medical art. Some of
the long bones of the body have been found that apparently were broken and creditably set so as to make
the member usable again.

Most of the medicines employed were simple herbs
but two of them at least were important contributions
to the modern art of healing. Quinine, which is extracted from the bark of the chinchona tree, was used
then as it is today to assist the body in breaking a fever.
Cocaine, prepared from the leaves of the cocaine bush,
was used as a narcotic. Unfortunately, the Spaniards
abused the use of this drug and broke the Incaic law by
giving it to the workers to deaden the pain and monot-

ony of endless labor. This one act probably did more to give the invaders complete and perpetual control over the natives than any one other. Today it is the cross that Peru must bear. No muleteer or workman will budge an inch without his daily ration of the deadening drug. The dream of every educated Indian of the Andean area is to eliminate from the daily life the use of cocaine and it is only when that dream is realized that the original inhabitants of the mountains will have again the strength to rule themselves and win back their lands.

4

Of all the cities found by the Spaniards, Cuzco was without a doubt the most awe-inspiring with its great temples and court yards. This city was the center of the official religion of the empire, Sun Worship. Although most of the Cuzco buildings were in some manner or form devoted to this religion or to the Inca's household, the worship of the Sun was not the only religion practiced even at the close of the Incaic period. In general, three types of worship were to be found throughout the area. The unintelligent lowest class of the people followed in the footsteps of their ancestors of ages past and practiced a fetish worship. This type of religion, if it may be so designated, is common to all very primitive people. All the higher religions have their ultimate roots in a fetish worship and there are few of them even today that are completely free of it. Primitive ignorant classes in the Inca empire thus worshiped natural phenomena and usually extremely crude images that represented them or spirits. This worship attempted to placate a supernatural order of beings that seemed to the worshipers to be working against them unless properly supplicated. This most primitive form of religion existed side by side in all the regions with a very high and intellectual type of worship directed toward a Creator-God, variously called Viracocha, Pachacamac or Con. The first of these names was common in the highlands. The second designation was used on the coast and the third, frequently associated with some suffix or prefix, in the extreme east. However, the fundamentals of the sects were the same.

From all the evidence that we have before us today, it appears that the Creator-God was worshiped as early as the time of the Tiahuanaco empire. In Incaic times and probably during the earlier period it was a religion of the intellectual people. It was adopted as a state religion by the Inca Viracocha who, as you will remember, had received a vision from this old Creator-God, that resulted in his being the Savior of the empire. It is quite probable that this show of strength was the leading factor in the adoption of the worship of the Creator-God by the Incas. In Cuzco, the site now occupied by the cathedral formerly held the special temple to Viracocha. The place of this form of worship in the official life of the ruler is rather interesting. The Incas claimed to have been descendants of the Sun and as such practiced

Sun Worship. After the adoption by Inca Viracocha of the worship of the Creator-God, Sun Worship was continued but with a totally different significance. It now became a reverence toward a power that was not all-mighty. It was more a proclamation of kinship with the Sun and, although there are far more temples for this official religion than for the latter one, it is believed that the monotheism of the Viracocha cult played a strong part in the worship of the intelligentsia during the last several reigns. It is explained that the Sun God was great but that there was an even higher and mightier God than the Sun, who was the Creator of everything. This was because the power of the Sun was not limitless. His face was obscured by the slightest of clouds. He was occasionally eclipsed by his mate, the Moon. At night it was impossible for him to show himself. In certain communities along the coast, the fact that the Moon could be seen both in the daytime and at night and that the Moon could and did eclipse the Sun caused that feminine figure, the Moon Goddess, to be exalted even above the Sun God.

Such a monotheism as the worship of Viracocha suggests may be found among almost all the higher civilizations in America. Most of them, as was true among the Incas, had a pantheon of lower deities who were by no means all-powerful nor free of human frailties but above all these, creating and directing the mechanics of the universe, was a single omnipotent force. Very frequently this force was not generally venerated but was a sort of god of the high priests, the lower castes worshiping the lesser gods who interceded for them with the All-High. We know most about the Sun Worship among the Incas. This is because at the time of the Conquest it was still the official religion of the Incas and was accompanied by a great show of ceremony that intrigued and often horrified the Spaniards.

The worship of the Sun was knit closely with the calendar. The Incas had not advanced so far as the Mayas and the related tribes in Mexico in developing a calendrical system. They did, however, have names for the lunar months and marked and celebrated the equinoxes and solstices. Outside of Cuzco there were two groups of towers that were used by the priesthood for determining those passages of the Sun. The Inca's year apparently began with the summer solstice and that month saw the greatest of the ceremonies, the solemn Feast of the Sun. At Cuzco, the seat of the government and religion, it was celebrated by rites conducted by the Inca and the High Priest of the Sun who was generally his uncle or brother. The minor rulers from all parts of the empire, accompanied by impressive troops and underlings, attended the ceremony. Each of the high dignitaries was gorgeously clothed in apparel representing his region. Those from the far east were swathed in robes made from the feathers of tropical birds, those from the coastal west in exquisitely wrought and decorated cotton. The powerful lords from the mountain regions wore robes made of puma fur. The feast proper was preceded by a three-day fast. During this period the Chosen Women, who were vestals to the Sun Temples, prepared the special maize bread to be used in the ceremony. During the same time the under-priesthood prepared the animals to be sacrificed in the rites. Before dawn on the day of the feast the Inca, accompanied by the important men of the nation, made his way to the great square east of the Temple of the Sun. There they all prostrated themselves, facing the rising deity. All the other guests to the ceremony assembled apart from those of imperial blood across the Rio Huatanay where they bowed to the rising Sun and could watch the Inca's ceremony. As the full disc glowed above the horizon the Inca arose and took two golden cups filled with maize beer. One of these he emptied as a libation to the Sun into a jar of gold from which the liquor flowed through a stone conduit to the Temple of the Sun. From the other cup he himself drank and what remained of his portion was divided among the other royal guests. This ceremony was the first of a long chain in worship of the Sun. The procession from there moved to the Sun Temple which was entered barefoot by everyone but the Inca. The two golden cups were presented to the priest in charge as gifts to the Sun. Each of the ruler chieftains then came forward and presented the many types of animals, modeled in gold and silver, found in his part of the realm. The presentation of tribute to the Sun God was followed by the formal sacrifice of a solid-black llama from the herds of the Sun, which was carried out by five priests. As among the ancient Mediterraneans, the condition and shape of the viscera of the sacrificed animal was used for augury. When this sacrifice had been completed a great many animals from the various flocks set aside for the Sun were sacrificed and set up as burnt offerings to the deity.

It is interesting to note how the Incas produced fire for this ceremony. The high priest wore on his left wrist a large bracelet that had on it a highly polished, concave plate of metal. This reflector was used to concentrate the rays of the Sun at one point where it ignited a tuft of cotton wool. If the day was so inauspicious as to be cloudy, when the Sun's power could not be called upon to light the sacrificial fire, the priests resorted to the friction method of rubbing sticks to get the spark. This was considered an extremely unlucky omen for it showed that the Sun was angry with his people and refused to give fire to them himself. The well-roasted flesh of the sacrificed animals and the sacred maize bread that had been made by the Chosen Women were then distributed to all the people present. This began the serious business of the day, feasting, and as the Sun moved through the sky the effects of good food and drinking bouts put the multitude into an uproarious condition.

The second month of the Inca year began during the last week of July. During it the irrigation systems were repaired and the fields plowed. The third month, which closed with the autumnal equinox, was the time of planting. A curious ceremony accompanied the seeding of the fields belonging to the Sun. Before the task was set upon, fifteen brown llamas from the Sun's herds were sacrificed at each of the holy places in the vicinity of Cuzco. The farmers then plowed the fields, accompanied by priests who performed special rites and who brought with them as a mascot a white llama ornamented with gold. These rites consisted primarily in pouring great libations of maize beer upon the soil. After the planting was finished, there was another period of sacrifice during which the Gods of Rain, Sleet and Thunder were placated.

The fourth month was devoted to ceremonies to the Moon, Viracocha and Chuqui-Illapa, the God of Thunder. These were primarily for relief from sickness, disaster, misfortunes and such perils. A part of the ceremony consisted in groups of warriors going out in the four directions of the compass and in the light of the Moon bathing in the rivers. It was thought that by such an action the nation was purified for the coming year and all that was harmful was carried by the rivers out of the domain.

During the fifth and sixth months most of the time was occupied in brewing maize beer and preparing the boys for maturity ceremonies to take place in the seventh month. The seventh month was ushered in by the winter solstice. This was the most important month of the year for the boys and girls who had reached maturity during the past twelve months. A very elaborate group of ceremonies was carried on to usher them into manhood and womanhood. Most of these were the concluding touches to their education which had been going on for some four years. The boys were engaged in feats of endurance and strength while the girls demonstrated their abilities in womanly ways. The entire affair was concluded when the Inca placed little golden pins in the pierced ear lobes of the boys, which act signified that they were to be accepted as men. During the following month, the newly armed warriors held a series of sham battles and exhibitions of their prowess for the multitude.

The ninth month, which came to an end on the spring equinox, was usually rainy and there were few rites held. The tenth and the eleventh months were devoted to preparing the crop for harvesting and to harvesting it, and the last month, which rounded out the year on the summer solstice, was celebrated with harvest festivals.

This is a greatly condensed schedule of the ceremonies carried on in the official religion, Sun Worship. There were many others and still more related to the other religions in vogue at the time. These ceremonies were for the most part attended and carried on solely by the aristocracy. The life of the lower classes was one with much less celebration and much more hard work.

5

With so much modern thought being expended on the pros and cons of communism, it is probably worth our time to study rather closely the earliest communistic state in the Americas of which we have any complete knowledge.

As we have seen, under the Inca rule the entire upland of Peru and most of the western coastal region was under the dominion of a small class of people. They ruled a population, made up of numerous different tribes of people, that numbered somewhere around thirty-five millions of souls at the height of their reign. The life of the ruling class was like that of any autocratic rulers but the attitude toward the people was quite different and, although they held their subjects with an absolute hand as all communistic leaders do, their plan of government was such that the greatest of care was afforded the common folks. Everything was highly organized and planned for the benefit of the community with full knowledge that what was good for the community was of greatest benefit to the ruler and his succession.

Let us take a small community and see how it was organized and what its people did for a living. All the land was public domain. No one owned property. Private ownership extended only to the tools of trade, which were crude and simple, and to the scant clothing and household goods of the family. Each landholder was given the use of about forty acres of ground, the produce from which was divided into three portions. One-third went for the use of the community and the landholder, one-third for the government and one-third for the Inca. In all probability the actual fields were not segregated but, as the population increased, more arable land was put under cultivation and the entire crop at the harvest time divided into its respective thirds. When there were increases in a family the usufruct of an additional forty acres was allotted to the head of the family if the child was a son and half that area if the child was a daughter. When the son married, he took with him the use of the land his parents had gained by his birth. When the daughter married, her land might remain with the family or be transferred to her husband. Upon the death of anyone for whom land had been assigned, the land reverted to the state.

In every community there are some who are not capable of tilling the soil and many who, though they are capable, should be relieved of that task because of other and more valuable attributes. Division of labor according to individual ability was established in the community under the rule of the Incas. The potter, the silversmith, the weaver and the sculptor, who were contributing to the glories of the nation with their skill, were supported wholly by the community and the land assigned to them was cultivated by the communal tillers of the soil. At the harvest time the third of the produce that was gathered first was assigned to the service of the

Sun; which, since the church and state were really one, meant that it was used to support the government, its employees and their families, the priesthood and the temples, the student priests and priestesses. The second third of the harvest belonged to the people of the community and the last to the ruling Inca. Of course, it was impossible for the Inca to use all the produce that was grown and gathered in his name. Thus great store houses were erected in each political division, where the Inca's surplus was hoarded away to be used for the relief of the communities in the vicinity during periods of stress and poor crops. Thus about one-third of a man's time, if he was an agriculturalist, was devoted to service for the state, one-third to service for the Inca and one-third for himself and the community.

The highly skilled craftsman was called upon to contribute an equal amount of time to the services of these three divisions. In each case, all that he supplied was his imagination and skill, his political rulers supplying him with the necessities of life and of his craft. So each citizen, if we may call him that, of the Inca empire devoted a large portion of his time to the state in one way and another. However, such state duties did not occupy all the time of the people. During the rest of the days in the year they were at liberty to work for themselves. Since people not versed in the art of ceramics might wish to acquire a bit of pottery and those who were efficient potters might produce more than they actually needed themselves, market places developed wherein, by means of barter, the excess handicraft of a family might be exchanged for desired goods. Such personal properties could not be claimed by the rulers or their minions.

In every community there are some people who are unable to carry on a normal existence—the old, the maimed, the blind. These were considered, along with orphans and widows, to be charges of the state and were supported wholly by the state. The division of labor in the community was based almost entirely on an age scale. Until the children were sixteen years old they played no part in the economics of the region but were dependent upon their parents. During this time they were occupied by a schooling that would fit them for their adult life. In the case of the hereditary ruling class, this schooling was a rigorous training for their social and political positions, including years of study of theology, history, languages and mathematics. After the boys or girls were sixteen years old, they spent the next four years under the tutelage of the older people of the village in learning a trade, whether it be that of an agriculturalist, a craftsman, a priest of the temple or a housewife. Between the years twenty and twenty-five they worked with their families and assisted them in their duties to the state. By the time they were twenty-five years old they were supposed to have been married and become landholders themselves. From then on until they were fifty, all the duties to the community and to the nation were upon their shoulders. Once they passed the half-century mark, they were relieved of this routine life and for the next ten years earned their keep in teaching the young. Persons of sixty or more were supported by the state and finished their lives at ease.

Of course, as in any state, there were duties to be performed that required mass labor, such as the building of roads or bridges, the building of temples, the carrying of messages, the care of herds that were the property of the state, and the defense of the country. For these services men were drafted to perform that part to which they were best adapted. The craftsman was exempt from any labor other than in his own particular field. The metalsmiths were called upon to do the decorative work in gold and silver, the masons to work in stone. The only exception to this was that every man was liable to call for the defense of the country and to herd the flocks of llama and vicuña that supplied the meat and wool for the nation.

All this required a well set up and completely controlled government which was headed by the Inca. The pyramid of authority built down from him to the head of each small community, whose duty it was to supervise the agriculture in his town. The well-being and contentment of the community was the full responsibility of this lowest division in the governmental hierarchy. One example from the laws that ruled the domain will show how heavily the responsibility rested upon these minor leaders. Theft was punishable by a public flogging. A second offense brought about a more severe and longer flogging and those who committed a third offense were considered incorrigible and detrimental to the community and therefore were killed. But if the theft was of food or the necessities of life and was brought about through the negligence of a governmental employee, that employee suffered the punishment and he who committed the theft was freed.

Few of the governmental positions were hereditary. Most of them were appointive and the incumbent removable at any time for cause. These conditions, together with the fact that the government employee was not taxed or called upon to contribute to the upkeep of the nation except with a portion of his time, and the fact that severe punishments would be meted out to him for failure to do his duty, all contributed to a smooth and efficient system of rule. As has been pointed out, the country was covered with a network of excellent highways along which at regular intervals were stationed rest houses and detachments of runners who, in an incredibly short time, could carry an order from the Inca in Cuzco to any part of his domain or bring him news therefrom. So, being in almost continual communication with all parts of his far-flung domain, the Inca ruler was able to rule effectively. In times of great emergency such as rebellion or attack from the outside, a system of signal fires was used which would carry the news across the breadth and length of the land in less than a day. These were most often employed in the case of attack by the warlike tribes to the north and the east.

Rebellion within the nation, until the advent of the Spaniards, was rare for a very simple reason. The Inca took exceedingly good care of his people and contented people don't rebel.

CHAPTER TEN

THE MOUND-BUILDERS

1

In the central part of North America there lived for
some time a group of people who have left us an immense number of examples of their architecture in the
form of mounds. Over most of the area they are literally
just that—great mounds of earth piled up like bread
loaf or conical in shape. In the northeastern area they
take the form of long fortifications as they have been
called, and in the northwestern are highly developed
into immense effigies of man and animals. Just who the
Mound-Builders of the Mississippi Valley were we
don't know. Certainly those in the north have every indication of a culture one stage in advance of that shown
by the Iroquois Indians who were met by the whites in
the early settlement of New York. Those in the south,
in Georgia and Alabama, although they had the same
complex for building mounds, were far more advanced
in the arts and, curiously, their decorative designs show
what has been termed a strong influx from Mexico.
This is particularly evident in repoussé work and in
carving on stone, in which the figures in feeling rather
than detail resemble those drawn by the Aztecs and

Mayas. Their pottery is well formed and decorated and resembles that from the southern part of Arizona and northern Mexico. Whether these artistic developments were indigenous or whether they were brought about through trading relations or whether there is a bare possibility of a true connection between the Mound-Builders of the south and the Mexican cultures must be decided in the future. The area covered extends from just north of the Great Lakes to the Gulf and from the westernmost region where corn could be grown without irrigation to the east coast as far north as Virginia and thence slightly westernly into western New York and the borders of the Lakes.

Just how long ago these people were building mounds is another question that must await the future. It has been partly answered by the work of Miss Florence Hawley in conjuncture with the Tennessee Valley Authority. There she has been able to date by means of the tree ring method the remains of several houses that probably were associated with a mountain fringe of the Mound-Builders and those dates fall into historic time. As yet they have not been made public. Of course, since the region is not typically Mound-Builder but rather represents an off-shoot such as might be expected on the periphery or as a relic, they mean very little except that in that region people with the complex for making huge piles of dirt were living at the time of the settlement of the east coast. That the Mound-Builders were not active throughout the major portion of their range at that time is evidenced by the lack of any mention of them in the accounts of the Spanish and French explorers of the Mississippi Valley. Many reasons have been set forth for their disappearance. But none of these have been postulated since Miss Hawley dated the structures in the Tennessee Valley. The evidence must be reconsidered before an adequate explanation can be forthcoming.

There is the possibility that one of the great southward migrations such as placed the Apaches and Navajos in the southwest may have brought warlike nomads into conflict with these more or less sedentary Plains Indians. That the Pueblo Indians managed to hold off the intruders may be credited to their easily defended cliff dwellings or stoutly built communal homes. The Mound-Builders were less well off and their culture may well have been destroyed. Without doubt some of the Plains tribes of historic time were descendants of the Mound-Builders.

From excavations that have been made during the past fifty years a great deal of information has been accumulated relative to the culture of these by-gone middle westerners. However, a full analysis has not been made and it will be attended, probably, with great difficulty when it is attempted since almost every small town in the Mound-Builder region has its local historical society and its collections of Mound-Builder material. Some of it, it seems to me, is acceptable data but most of it is of no practical use for archeological studies. Yet it must be seen and taken into account before a full picture can be drawn. The Ohio region, which is particularly rich, has been well studied and Dr. Shetrone has given us the only recent account of the Mound-Builders, which is excellent as far as it goes.

Careful studies of the mounds that have been dissected have led scientists to believe that one of the prime uses was as a place of burial. A great many of them show in their centers a cremation pit containing the fragments of bones of one or more skeletons. Others are monuments above interments in a second type of burial. It is quite possible that the bodies were first exposed and when nothing remained but the whitened bones these were gathered together and placed in the base of a mound. In some cases a log charnel house was built and, after it was used, covered with a great pile of dirt. Like the pyramids of Yucatan, a number of the mounds show successive periods of building and in their dissection three and sometimes four stages are discernible. It may be that these burial mounds represent the earliest type and that those raised apparently for no reason at all, a later type. Certainly burials are rare, if not entirely absent, in the effigy mounds, which are surely a later development, and in the fortification mounds. The theory has been formulated that the mounds were built as places of refuge in time of flood. This applies very well to those situated close to the Mississippi and to its giant tributaries. However, a great many of them are in such position that they could by no means have served this purpose. I am afraid that we will not be able to ascribe any real reason to the building of mounds. It seems to be just an expression of the American trait of piling up dirt or rocks into high buildings. There must be something in the air for even we, who are of European extraction, have emulated the aborigines in making our buildings taller and taller.

2

The Mound-Builder area is divided by archeologists into several regions. These regions are by no means clear-cut anywhere but on the map. As a matter of fact, the whole so-called Mound-Builder culture is in such a state at present that it will take a lifetime or more before any satisfactory analysis of the people, their habits and productions can be made. Probably the most thoroughly known and best studied region is that centering in the state of Ohio, the home of the famous Hopewell culture and several minor ones. In the northwest, in Wisconsin, Minnesota and the Dakotas, and straggling down as far south as the center of Missouri is an area called the Upper Mississippi region. This is a region with considerable mixture of remains with different cultural characteristics, some of them from the east and some of them from the far south. The area from St. Louis to the Gulf in the Mississippi Valley con-

stitutes the Lower Mississippi culture and the lower half
of that alone seems to be fairly uniform. The upper half
exhibits many intrusions of cultural characteristics that
are dominant in Wisconsin or Ohio. The mounds of
Florida constitute a fairly pure cultural group. Through
the foothills of the Appalachian highlands in Tennessee
and Kentucky is found the Cumberland association of
Mound-Builders. These remains frequently reveal a
mixture of Ohio and Mississippi Valley characteristics.
The mounds of western New York, northwest Pennsylvania, the peninsula of Michigan and the southern part
of Ontario in Canada have been designated as belonging
to the Great Lakes cultural region. Of this area really
very little is known and it is quite possible that many of
the mounds are remains left us by Algonkian and Iroquois Indians. As a matter of fact, there is more than a
suspicion that these two groups may be a residue of the
former extensive Mound-Builder people that inhabited
the northern part of the Great Plains area and Mississippi Valley. The Lower Mississippi Mound-Builders
may have been the ancestors of the Creeks and other
southern tribes.

Since so much confusion reigns among the specialists
who have studied extensively the works of these by-
gone people, it is probably best here not to attempt a
summary of the entire region but to pick three or four
outstanding and characteristic groups of mounds and
describe briefly what has been found in the exploration
of them.

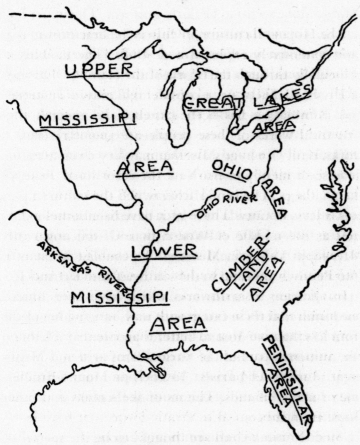

THE MOUND-BUILDER REGION

3

The Hopewell culture of Ohio is the best known and most extensively explored and studied of all. There, principally through the efforts of the State of Ohio and of Dr. H. C. Shetrone, a considerable mass of material and information has been gathered. In general, the structural works of these people are geometric earthworks, built on a huge scale, that may have been used for defense or merely to mark off the ceremonial areas in their villages. The center from which the culture radiates is Ross County. Traces of it have been found as far west as the middle of Wisconsin and well down the Mississippi Valley in Missouri. To the east it extends into Pennsylvania and to the southeast into Kentucky.

In addition to earthworks which have been found one hundred acres in extent with walls ranging in height from less than one foot to better than twenty feet, there are numerous tumuli of various shapes that contain great numbers of burials. An enclosure may surround one or many mounds. The mounds themselves vary in shape from subconical to erratic forms that have been likened to animals and are thought to be the source of the great effigy mounds of Wisconsin. These huge piles of dirt were built laboriously by carrying baskets of dirt, frequently from distant places, and heaping them up on a specially prepared surface. This preparation consisted in removing all the vegetation and the top soil. The subsurface was then treated with a thick layer of carefully

spread clay. On this clay surface fine sand and gravel
was put down as the top dressing, often to the depth of
several inches. The prepared floor served as the surface
for the building of what may be altars, for crematory
basins and burial pits. Quite frequently the sanded area
was surrounded by a palisade, the post holes and stubs
of which are still evident. On it were erected small
wooden structures used as charnel houses which, after
they had served their purpose, were burned probably
in some purifying rite and then covered with mounds of
dirt, the ultimate accumulation of which formed the
tumuli which we know today. The crematory basins, or
burial pits, were usually constructed of carefully pud-
dled clay. Many of them show extensive use, the ground
beneath them being oxidized to a considerable depth.

It is interesting to note that two forms of burial were
common in this phase of the Mound-Builder culture.
By far the majority of the dead were cremated but a few,
possibly those who were religious and secular leaders in
the community, were buried on low platforms of clay,
their bodies fully extended and accompanied by great
quantities of artifacts, many of them of high beauty. In
the case of cremation it is evident that the procedure
was to remove the ashes of the deceased from the crematory basin and place them in a much smaller clay pit
together with offeratory implements. These implements
tell the story of extensive travel and trade on the part
of the people. Obsidian tools that were probably made
of stone brought from the Rocky Mountain region in

the form of great chunks of that volcanic glass are found commonly distributed through the Ohio area. Accompanying one burial which was probably that of a master artisan are huge chunks of the precious stuff and a great pile of partially worked flint and rejected chips. When it is realized that the material must have been trekked through all kinds of country for one thousand miles or more on the backs of men, this cache represents a tremendous sacrifice on the part of the community to do honor to the man whose burial it accompanied. Occasionally the burial pits were lined with flat plates of mica, a substance greatly prized by these people for decorative purposes. Most frequently, however, the pits were not lined and the little piles of ashes from each cremation merely heaped here and there on the clay surface. The extended uncremated burials usually carry far more interesting loot for the archeologist. One of them in which a man and woman were buried is of particular interest and I quote its description from Dr. Shetrone's book, "The Mound-Builders."

"Lying side by side in a common grave, extended upon their backs, were the skeletons of a male and a female, both of them comparatively young. That of the male indicated an individual of nearly six feet in height and of striking massiveness and muscularity. The accompanying skeleton indicated a comely young female of medium size. Both were richly bedecked with ornaments, the double burial being an imposing example of barbaric splendor. At the head, neck, hips and knees of the female and completely surrounding the skeleton were thousands of pearl beads and buttons of wood and stone covered with copper; extending the full length of the grave along one side was a row of copper ear ornaments; on the wrists of the female were copper bracelets; copper ear ornaments adorned the ears of both and both wore necklaces of grizzly bear canines and copper breast plates on the chest. Lying across the collar bone of each skeleton from points beneath the ears to about the lower extremity of the breast bone, were copper rods, about one foot long, on which apparently the hair had been secured. Strangest of all, each skull was equipped with an artificial nose of copper. The copper noses were decidedly post-mortem insertions, and a plausible explanation of them would be that the Hopewell builders, especially familiar with human anatomy, realizing that the nasal appendage decomposes quickly after death, supplied this young couple with imperishable noses that they might not pass into the beyond lacking these useful and ornamental features."

In general, this type of burial is accompanied by much copper, mica and pearl ornamental material, the copper usually worked into breast plates and helmets, the pearls in the form of necklaces often with three hundred or more of the gems in a single string and the mica exquisitely cut into decorative designs laid upon the body. The preserving action of the copper breast plates has left to us small remnants of cloth that resembles a

COPPER ORNAMENT
Mound City, Ohio
(After Shetrone)

MICA ORNAMENT
Hopewell Culture. Ohio
(After Shetrone)

coarse homespun. Some of this bears designs in brown, yellow and dark red. Many of the male burials are accompanied by skulls or lower jaws that show clearly the marks of stone knives that have been used in cleaning them of their flesh. The jaw bones are almost universally perforated and it is supposed that they were worn around the neck as a sort of pendant. Whether these were trophies of war or ancestral relics we don't know. Of course, it is quite probable that they may represent both types of property.

That the Ohio Mound-Builders had at least some commerce with the people on the gulf coast is evidenced by the appearance of ornaments made from the shells of the marine turtle and from the jaws of the barracuda, a tropical fish.

In the same region there occurs what is called the Fort Ancient culture. Just what relationship this horizon bears to the Hopewell culture is not clear at present although many indications point to it as the forerunner. One habit of these people gives us a considerable insight into the life of the villages. Their idea of public sanitation was extremely curious. In and around their houses they allowed the debris from kitchens and the general life to accumulate until apparently they could no longer stand the sight and odor of it. They then proceeded to carry baskets full of dirt in from the surrounding region and bury the malodorous village. This repeated covering up of the surface gradually raised the ground level until the last occupied was several feet above the earliest.

The archeologists exploring such a site get a beautiful cross section of the food and general utensils used in the villages. From such explorations we have discovered that maize, as in the rest of America, was the principal food stuff. In addition to this the usual beans

and squash appear to have been cultivated. A great
many of the wild plants, particularly berries and nuts,
formed a part of the diet of these people. Tobacco apparently was a crop almost as important as corn and it seems
to have been used for general smoking in either stone or
clay pipes and in the religious ceremonies. The bones
scattered through the debris show us that the hunters

BIRD-PIPE FROM TREMPER MOUND, OHIO
(After Shetrone)

brought in for food practically all of the wild animals
abundant in the region—deer, turkey, bear, opossum,
raccoon and many other of the smaller, less easily identified animals and birds. Great accumulations of fish
bones and mussel shells are evidence of no mean ability
at fishing. The bones of many animals were fashioned
into fish hooks, needles, bodkins, awls and even hoes.
The teeth of the bear were particularly prized for necklaces. Some pottery was made, rather well shaped but
decorated only with simple incised geometric designs.

The clothing consisted primarily of skins and a small amount of cloth woven from vegetable fibers, animal

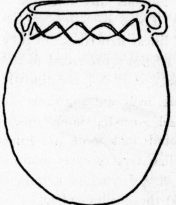

hairs and feathers. This early culture does not seem to have used much copper for implements or decoration. Almost all their tools were made of stone or bone and their body ornaments of shell, bone beads and perforated stones.

4

POT AND PIPE, FEURT SITE, OHIO
(From Photo by Shetrone)

The upper basin of the Mississippi River contains a branch of the Mound-Builder culture that, although it is found occasionally in other regions, seems to center in Wisconsin. These builders developed to a high degree the effigy mounds. Such structures are almost always associated with both linear and conical mounds of small size. The works of this group differ from that of the Hopewell culture in the total absence of enclosures or fortification walls. The linear mounds are usually quite straight, not serpentine as in the more eastern region and occasionally attain a length of one thousand feet. A curious development is seen in a combination of the linear and the conical mounds that resemble a chain of low cones of earth. There are a few erratic combinations of conical and linear structures but they are rather rare. Among the effigies represented in the Wisconsin area we find hawks, swallows, occasionally geese, buffalo, bear, deer, fox, wolf and a curious object that has been designated a turtle, though many of these so-called turtle mounds look more like huge war clubs. Probably the earliest type of effigy mound, of which there are a very few, is that of a human being. Time has so softened the outlines of many of the earthworks that it is quite impossible to decide just what they represent and in many cases even those that are in good condition and not badly eroded must be drawn out on paper after a survey before their symmetry and beauty can be recognized. At Mendota, Wisconsin there is probably the largest of these effigy mounds, a huge hawk or eagle with a wing spread of six hundred and twenty-four feet. There are no very high structures in the region. Some of them are piled scarcely two feet above the normal surface of the land. Others range as high as twenty feet. It is only to the south in the area of inundation that really high mounds are found.

There is a great difference in the method of burial in this region compared with that of the Hopewell culture. In the Ohio mounds burials are found scattered throughout the entire structure. In the effigies they are located in the position that would be occupied by the heart of the beast represented. In the case of the conical mounds that are associated with this group of people

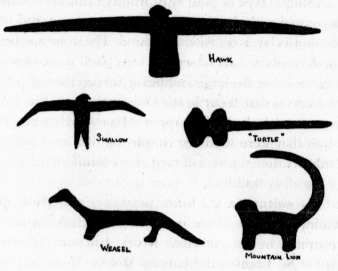

EFFIGY MOUNDS
(From Outlines by Shetrone)

the burials are found in exactly the center of the mound. Both cremated and extended burials occur. In addition, bundle burials are not infrequent. In this type of interment the bones of the deceased are gathered up after the flesh has fallen away and bundled together for burial. Many of the cremated burials among the effigy builders are found on rude small altars in the earth-work and there is just a bare possibility that such burials were sacrificial or at least associated with the ceremony of dedicating the mound. In the Hopewell culture a great deal of the handicraft of the people is found associated with the remains of the deceased. Here in Wisconsin artifacts are far less common.

A simple type of pottery of wholly utilitarian shapes, decorated with designs made by impressing a cord into the moist clay, is occasionally found. The stone and bone implements are all of service ware and, to my knowledge, none of the large and beautiful ceremonial points and knives that occur in the lower portion of the valley are found here in the upper Mississippi basin. The pipes that were used are simple and made of pottery. Only occasional pieces of copper are found in the graves of the effigy builders.

The culture in the lower portion of the Mississippi Valley seems to divide itself into two clear-cut phases separated by the Arkansas River. Just outside of the city of St. Louis is the famous Monks' Mound. There has been very little scientific excavation in the type of culture represented by the Monks' Mound. There have been a goodly number of interesting things dug up by amateurs but unfortunately very little of this material has sufficient information about its actual source to be of any importance in putting together the puzzle of the Mound-Builders. The University of Illinois, some six or seven years ago, carried on for several years intensive exploration of this group, known as the Cahokia group. The largest mound of the area is Monks' Mound. It measures 1080 feet by 710 feet and is about 100 feet high. It is built in four terraces, the topmost of which supported a ceremonial lodge of some sort or other. The lower terraces show signs of having been used for living purposes and there are the remains of more than a few houses.

As yet the burial place of these people has not been found and until it is we will probably know little of the arts and crafts practiced by them. In the occasional inhumations that have been found there have accompanied the burial some rather fine examples of pottery. In the debris piles that usually occur in such villages, in addition to traces of the foodstuffs used by the people, there has come to light a typical triangular arrow point that seems to be characteristic of the phase of the Mound-Builder culture represented at Cahokia. This point is about two and a half times as long as it is wide, with straight sides and very deeply serrate edges. Such flint chipping is easily recognized and through it a small ground of mounds in Wisconsin have been recognized as belonging to this sect.

Further south in Missouri there lived a small group of people who built stone vaults as burial chambers in which have been found both cremated and uncremated remains. These stone vault people were far better potters than any of the Mound-Builders living north of their region. The bowl shapes resemble the Mexican wares far more closely than anything that has been produced or found in the Pueblo region of the southwestern states. Many of the bowls are eared with effigies of animals, the head at one side and the tail at the other. The sides are frequently decorated with a combination

of incised designs that have been filled in with paint. Associated with the burials have been found several beautiful shell gorgets with amazing designs engraved upon them. Several of these show a human figure that at first glance is quite Aztec in costume and execution. However, a closer study shows no absolutely true Aztec characteristic in the workmanship. It is merely a superficial resemblance but one that is strikingly clear.

So. Missouri Painted Water Jug and Incised Effigy Bowl
(From Photos by Holmes)

South of the Arkansas River there are a great many mounds. However, it will be probably some time before they are excavated systematically and studied. The great difficulty in doing this work is getting permission from the owners to take down a mound and study its structure. The mounds are used today for probably the same purpose as their original builders intended—places

MOUND-BUILDERS' POTTERY
From Lower Mississippi
After Moore

of refuge in the time of flood. A good many of them have farm houses situated on the top and not a few have been used for modern cemeteries. All this will add to the confusion when the future archeologist attempts to analyze his find and synthesize the culture of the original builders. When it was discovered by the present inhabitants of the area that the pottery contained in the old burials had value there was a deluge of it on practically every local merchant and many a man paid off his bills with the ceremonial ware of this by-gone race.

It is here that we find the very best of the effigy pottery that has been produced in North America and associated with it a type of water bottle that is reminiscent of southwestern Mexico—squat bottles with long slender necks. The decoration on these and on the bowls is again a combination of incision and painting. The designs used are developments of scrolls, a modified swastika and what may be highly conventionalized flower patterns. Among them occurs the almost exact replica of the sun symbol used by the state of New Mexico as its seal which, in turn, was derived from the sun symbol of the Indians living in the vicinity of Mexico City in the days of the Spanish Conquest. It is in this region that we find the only tripod pots, the hollow legs of which contain rattle pellets as in the Archaic Horizon in the Valley of Mexico. There are several curious design motifs used by these people. A type of pot usually referred to as a funiary vase often bears a decoration consisting of the extended hand in the back of which is set an eye. Another group of pots supposedly used for the same purpose are decorated with skulls and long bones. Curiously enough, the ramus of the lower jaw is drawn protruding beyond the skull just as it was drawn by the primitive tribes of Central Mexico. The rattlesnake design is found on other bowls but much more frequently on plaques or gorgets. Occasionally pieces of shell work have been found in which the snake is very distinctly plumed. The use of the plumed serpent has been considered to be an indication of contact with either the Maya or the Aztec people from Central America. Such design was used rarely by the Hopis and the Zunis in the Southwest. I feel that it is not beyond the realm of possibility that Maya traders reached the Gulf coast states and introduced a good many characteristics of their art in the form of trade ware and that the potters and engravers who were living there took a fancy to the Mexican wares and designs and made them for their own use.

A goodly number of the skulls that have been recovered from burials in the Gulf states are deformed. This deformation is not like that found among the Pueblo Indians who flattened the back of the head, but more like that found among the Mayas where the compression occurred on the forehead and caused the head to grow upward and backward, almost conical. All these Mexican influences or apparent influences increase rather than decrease the puzzling nature of the Mound-Builder culture in the Mississippi Valley.

There are two other cultural regions that are worthy of a word or two. To the east in the Cumberland Mountains of Tennessee a great many small settlements that were inhabited probably by mound building people have been found. During the last year in clearing the mounds of the Tennessee Valley Authority Project these have been thoroughly studied. The wood found in the house ruins has been preserved and a tree ring chronology erected from modern times back to the time of habitation of these villages; and, as has occurred whenever actual reliable dates have been arrived at for the antiquities in America, they are surprisingly recent. Apparently the Cumberland area was occupied during the 14th and 15th centuries. It is to be hoped that Miss Hawley, to whom must go the honor for having arrived at a dating system for this region, will be able to extend her studies to the other mound building regions, at least those in Ohio, and actually date such characteristic structures as are found in the Hopewell ruins.

5

On the peninsula of Florida along the east coast have been found a great many artificial islands built up of shells. From these have been recovered a number of extraordinary pieces of wood carving. Unfortunately, no suitable method has been devised as yet to prevent these works of art from warping and splitting into pieces when they are removed from the muck in which they lie buried. Masks, animal effigies and beautifully wrought *atlatl* sticks have been found. At first glance, the material is strikingly like that of the coastal tribes found in British Columbia and southern Alaska. However, the

WOODEN MASK
Key Marco, Fla.
(After Cushing)

skeletal and cultural material recovered indicate that the people who built these shell islands were related to and probably the remnants of the early inhabitants of the Lesser Antilles, the Arawak and Carib Indians. I fear that to go into the remains of this interesting region any further would be to wander afield from the purpose of this summary.

CHAPTER ELEVEN

AMERICA'S CONTRIBUTION

1

To many persons archeology is a useless pursuit, yet funds are made available annually for its study. It is one of the few sciences that involves no gain in the grossest sense of the word, yet every item of archeological discovery is all gain in piecing together the historical background of the human race. Its study is completely satisfying to the all-consuming curiosity of mankind. Nothing seems more important to us than our ancestry, so year after year men continue to expend great energy and considerable funds of money to satisfy that curiosity.

The study of antiquities in the Americas has lagged far behind similar studies in Europe. This can be excused to some extent since we have been busy during the last 400 years in converting these continents into a satisfactory place for Europeans to live in. Although American archeology is still very young, it is a lusty infant and much has been added to the sum of knowledge through its study, but what we have learned is hardly an atom compared with what is still to be uncovered.

To be sure, there are certain phases about which we

have a satisfying knowledge, but the lacunae between them are great. For instance, thus far all discoveries of really primitive man in the Americas have been fragments of skeletons that indicate those ancient ones to have been the modern type of man which you and I represent. There have been no discoveries of individuals that might be considered "missing links" in the chain of stages through which man must have passed.

This brings up the question—could modern man have originated on these western continents or did he come here from the Old World? The answer that he is an immigrant from the Old World, which is given so promptly, is beginning to be given with less assuredness. We are approaching a state where we do not know. The sparse evidence that has been gathered together would indicate that one of two changes in our present thought must be made. Either we must revise our time concept as it applies to the geology of the Americas, or we must accept modern man as having been an inhabitant of these continents before he resided in Europe. Either of these hypotheses seems repugnant at present. To condense the last 100,000 years of geological history in the Americas to 20,000 years seems impossible. Such a revision is not at all compatible with what we earnestly feel to be the truth. The events of these later millennia in earth history have shown America to be parallel to Europe in the changes that took place. However, in recent years the discovery of dateable ruins underlying heavy deposits of volcanic ash in the Southwest has brought to our attention how recently the great earth forces have been active in our country. If we accept the second choice, that modern man has not changed very much in his hundred-thousand-year life in America, it postulates much too long a time without cultural advancement to be compatible with our vanity. And yet at present it seems as though those are the two theses between which we must make a choice.

But there is a third possibility which is purely hypothetical and has no real support, only tenuous chance. Maybe man did develop in his modern form on the Americas, and at the time when such mammals as the camel, the horse and the elephant deserted the New World, he followed them, since they were the source of his livelihood, and then returned to America in later ages after he had conquered Europe and Asia. Such a supposition is sheer blasphemy upon the ears of most students of mankind, but it is a possibility.

2

Now what has been contributed in a positive way through the study of the pre-Columbian people in the Americas or by those people themselves? The persistent idea that the Indians were solely hunters and fishers is quite erroneous, a mistaken notion for which there is no support in the reports upon the conditions of the country made by its earliest explorers. The ancient civilizations were all of agricultural people, and their contributions to the world diet have been far greater than the layman generally recognizes. To begin with their diet lacked any vegetable food in common with the peoples of the Old World. Just as the Asiatic peoples might be said to represent a rice civilization, the American Indians had a maize civilization. Wherever they tilled the soil efficiently, their staple agricultural product was maize. In the northern parts of the Canadian Great Plains region they grew a type that matured with amazing rapidity during the short summers of that land. In the south their plantations grew a variety of types that seem ideally suited for the conditions under which they were cultivated.

In discussing the Basket-Makers on p. 39 I remarked that the supposed progenitor of maize is the *teocintli* grass of the Valley of Mexico. Many botanists have expressed the opinion that this generally accepted supposition is erroneous but have had no suggestions to take its place. It appears now that they will have support for their contention. During recent explorations in the jungle of Guatemala Indians brought to the men of the Tulane University expedition several kernels of a grain that greatly resembles maize. The grain is not maize as we know it today but is very suggestive of what a wild ancestor of it might be like. The men were told that the grain grows as a grass and that each plant produces a very few seeds. Proposed botanical exploration of this region may result in settling the age-long problem of the wild ancestor of primitive America's most important agricultural product.

But maize is not the only contribution, nor to Europeans is it the most important one to the diet of the people. The white potato which has become the basic item in the diet of most of the European peasantry is an America food imported, over a devious route, from the highlands of Peru. The southeastern states of our own country contributed the sweet potato and the tropical lands the closely related yams. Tobacco is another American product without which the world today would be at somewhat of a loss. All of the beans except the soy-bean and the horse-bean and all varieties of squash and pumpkin were agricultural products first seen by the Europeans in the gardens of the American Indians. Watermelons, now grown in many places in the world, were without doubt a contribution from this continent. All the evidence that has been proposed supporting the theory that this peculiar fruit is of Asiatic or Egyptian origin seems lacking in force. The bitter melon of Egypt does resemble the watermelon, but students of agriculture are convinced that it could not have been the ancestor of our product.

A full list of the contributions made to the world's table by the New World would require a volume of its own. Let me just add a few more of the garden products that had their original home here. Garden peppers, tomatoes, bananas, cassava were all cultivated in the

American tropics. Many of the wild berry plants upon which we depend today were used in their wild state in ancient times. Strawberries, black raspberries, blackberries and gooseberries are a few of the more common of these. Of medicinal plants there are many—cascara, quinine and cocaine are all products that were first used by the aborigines in the Americas. The cotton grown here is botanically different from that of Asiatic origin and the so-called Egyptian or Sea-Island cotton, noted for its long fibers, was first grown upon the American coast.

In the matter of domestic animals the Americas were far behind the Old World. The dog, man's ever present companion, was bred here for food, its wool, the hunt and without doubt its companionship. This animal is the only living thing that the cultures of the Old World and the New World had in common other than man himself. In North and Central America the turkey, the largest of the barnyard fowl, was domesticated. In the Andes the ancient civilizations had flocks of three curious closely related animals that belong to the camel type—the vicuña and the alpaca for their wool and the llama for its meat and possibly as a beast of burden. In North America no large animal had been domesticated; the only member of the bovine type, the bison, is temperamentally unfit for domestication, though it did supply much of the meat used by the nomadic tribes of the Middle West at the time of the arrival of the whites.

3

Agricultural civilizations are usually pottery civilizations. This stands to reason since the manufacture and use of pottery is hardly suited to a people who are constantly on the move, such as those that compose a nomadic hunting and fishing community. Thus it should not be surprising to find the distribution of pottery in the Americas about the same as that of well-developed agriculture.

In certain regions where source materials were easily available other types of utensils were more commonly used, but hardly ever to the exclusion of pottery vessels. A good example is to be seen among the Iroquois Nations—a semi-agricultural people who inhabited what is now Ontario and New York. They utilized the easily peeled bark of the birch tree to form vessels that were sewed with sinews and sealed with pine pitch, in addition to pottery.

We are fortunate to have a rather complete picture of the development of pottery in the Americas through the various stages from its inception to the exquisitely formed portrait and pictorial wares of some of the Peruvian civilizations. In the southwestern states, New Mexico and Arizona, the archeologists have found examples of clay vessels that represent the very beginning of the art. These, you will remember, were formed by molding plastic clay in a basket and burning away the basket. This, like all great inventions, probably came about in an accidental way. From there on we are able to trace the development of hard, fired pottery through its many stages.

The early manufacturers of true pottery first produced only those shapes that were necessary in the routine duties of their primitive households—water jugs, shallow bowls for the storage of seeds, cooking pots and the like. This stage in the development of the art is most completely presented for us in the culture that succeeded the Basket-Makers, the Pueblo culture.

A study of their pottery reveals that the first development, after a satisfactory method for making articles had been achieved, was the application of decoration to the article. The decoration may be simple scratches forming an incised pattern, or paints applied to the smooth surfaces of the utensil. Early in the history of Pueblo pottery the makers selected the paint technique as their mode of decoration. At first, when the vessels were small, the applied designs were painted on the inside of the product. Gradually as the vessels made became larger, the design extended to the outside until eventually there was little or no ornamentation on the inner surface and the entire outer surface was covered.

The use of paints and slips has been discussed previously. The designs themselves are for the most part simple geometric combinations. Toward the close of the Pueblo period there appears to have been a movement to use life motifs in the decoration. These had not become highly stylized before the culture began to decline and the advent of the Spaniards prevented the normal upward surge that should have followed the period after the Great Drought.

In the Archaic horizons of Mexico we can follow the development of pottery through its next stage. In it the design remains rather simple and stylized while the shapes of the vessels seem to pass through a great sequence of modification. This period introduces a clear-cut separation of the wares made for purely utilitarian purposes and those associated with the ceremonies of religion. Accompanying this ceremonial ware are the figurines that are ever present in cultural horizons that show distinctive ceremonial wares and doubtless are linked closely with the religious expression of the people who made them.

It is to be expected that the next stage in the development of pottery should be one in which the shapes have become highly developed and rather stagnant, and the decoration highly stylized. This is true of the later civilizations in Mexico. Recent explorations in the central part of Middle America on the southern fringe of the Maya territory have brought to light several hundred perfect specimens of pottery that startlingly fulfill this supposition. Here we find minutely detailed designs appearing on strongly fixed shapes. The association of a particular pattern with a particular type of vessel is so universal in the collections made in the Uloa Valley that it is possible to reconstruct an entire pot from a single small sherd. Such extraordinary relationship indicates that the art was on the verge of decadence. The discovery of alabaster bowls with similar shapes strengthens the idea. The craftsmen had arrived at a point where at least for a time they must employ their talents in another medium before the inspiration for further development of pottery would take place.

The ceramic remains found along the northern coast of Peru indicate a further development in the art on the American continent. Here we see, in its highest degree, effigy ware. The portraits and domestic scenes modeled by the Chimu potters have never been equaled anywhere in the world. A further development of pottery never took place.

The period of stylization and decadence that followed the Chimu was a long one and it seems that again the Spaniards' arrival in the 16th century prevented the natural development of new techniques. In the Old World we can see what might have happened in the Americas. Apparently the natural advance would have been to apply a high glaze to pottery objects and then finally to combine with this beautifully glazed ware the use of very carefully selected clays for the production of porcelain. In China the potters reached that ultimate stage in their craft.

With continued explorations in the well-known regions of the Old World, archeologists have discovered that the art of pottery making has passed through essentially the same stages there as it did on our shores. Those stages, however, belong to a remote time in history. Simple bowl forms decorated on the inside, not unlike the wares produced during the first Pueblo stage, date back to about 5000 B. C. in Egypt and belong to the Badarian horizon.

Recent discoveries at Susa in Persia have revealed a similar type of pottery that has been ascribed to the later years of the fourth millennium before Christ. Similarly the pottery made by the ancient Chinese as early as 3000 B. C., and in Palestine during King Solomon's time, resemble each other in their general form and mode of decoration. These compare so well with the fine pottery of the Pueblo III period that archeologists may be confused by samples of the Old and the New World art. The subtle differences used in carrying out the designs are just evident enough to prevent Old World pieces from being referred to a center of production in this country.

The use of decoration imprinted by means of the finger or thumb nail, such as is found in any refuse heap in the Southwest, was common in Spain during the culture period known as Inner Catalan. The workmanship and the products of the potters who lived in England during the Late Neolithic times closely resemble the early incised ware of Archaic Mexico. The fine painted pottery from the Uloa Valley in Honduras has its counterpart in the beautiful painted Greek ware of early times.

I could go on almost indefinitely showing similar developments in form, design and technique between the early ceramics of the Old World and the New World. Essentially we may say that the developments are parallel and that the Old World counterparts are products of a time ranging from 1000 to 5000 years earlier. This similarity has been noted by many students of art and by some has been thought to indicate that in the New World the craft is a direct derivative from the Old World. I fail to follow their reasoning. The majority of the students of man feel that this is merely another example of the logical development in arts and crafts expressed wherever man makes his home. It is an example of the really narrow confines of human thought and ingenuity. I suppose that, had the high civilizations of Middle and South America been left undisturbed, they would, by the close of the 30th century, have equaled the fine porcelains that represent the acme of achievement by the Chinese potters.

That the American Indians could not have inherited their ceramics from the Old World is perfectly evident. From their agricultural products we know that they arrived here as immigrants fom Asia at a non-agricultural stage in their development. Since pottery and agriculture are so intimately linked, it is foolhardy to consider that these wanderers introduced the art of working in clay before they had any use for the products that it would produce.

If we consider that man progresses the world over at approximately the same rate, once he has become established as a husbandman, then we can use the stage to which the development of pottery had extended as a rough time-bearer in regard to man's sedentary inhabitation of a particular region. Applying such a yard stick in the New World we find that it would indicate that man has been settled for the longest periods of time on the Peruvian and Middle American coasts. Since their work compares favorably in all respects with that of early Greeks, we might further state that they were only ten or twelve centuries behind that Old World area in development. On the other hand the pottery that was being produced toward the end of the first Christian millennium in the Southwest would indicate a lag of 5000 years behind the oldest civilizations in the Mediterranean Basin.

If the region from which the present races of men disseminated is central Asia, the distances they must have traveled to establish themselves on the warm shores on the Mediterranean on one hand, and the similarly warm shores of the Caribbean on the other hand, are not very different. It is not impossible that both areas were settled at about the same time. We must suspect then that the long trek through the cold Sub-Arctic in some way affected the constitution of the early arrivals in America so that they were much slower in creating pottery. If for a minute we examine the possibility of such an occurrence, it will become evident that that might be the case. The active inventive individual is highly sensitive to his surroundings. He would have been at an extreme disadvantage during the westerly and then southerly migration through the cold regions where stolidity would serve as a paramount virtue in ignoring the long dark winters and the barren country. It is doubtful if a sensitive individual could have survived to maturity under such conditions. Thus the migration of ancient Americans was beset with ordeals that eliminated from the population all but the plodding and stolid element, and the inventions that caused civilization to stride forward were necessarily delayed until there had developed a sufficient strain of sensitive individuals to make the forward steps.

4

As with pottery, it is possible to trace the development of social institutions on the American continent; and in them too there is a close parallel between the New and the Old World. Religion developed here along the well-established lines of religion in the Mediterranean area. If Christianity had not been forced upon the native population, they themselves would soon have developed a monotheism. At the time of the conquest of the western hemisphere by the various nations of Europe, the country was a grand picture of all stages in the development of religious thought. The primitive nomadic peoples of the colder extremes in the temperate zones were practicing the lowest form—animism. They were worshiping natural phenomena with fear. Each catastrophe that occurred was the wrath of some evil spirit against man. These evil spirits had not yet attained the dignity of gods but inhabited every natural object and seemed to wait in ambush to attack some trembling human. In order to placate these forces the primitive people offered the products of their harvest and hunt to the spirits with the hope of being overlooked in the future.

Slowly there developed certain individuals who gained the reputation of communing with these spirits and were therefore able to assist or destroy their neighbors. Such was the foundation of a priesthood. When man settled down to an agricultural life, he soon observed that certain of these forces were now more important to him than were others. It was those that controlled rain and snow, heat and cold and the development of seed, whose favor he must curry in order that his crops might be spared. It was not long before this line of thought developed a definite religion catering to the agricultural gods. In its simplest form portions of the produce were set aside as offerings at the close of a harvest. Occasionally sacrifices were employed at the sowing season to insure the good will of the gods during the development of crops. As this progressed, worship of the deities became so involved that it was necessary that a specific group of men take it upon themselves to carry out the numerous ceremonies called for. Just as soon as a distinct class grew up to act as intermediaries between the layman and the gods, it is to be expected that a highly elaborate worship would evolve. The priesthood had to have a good reason for its continued existence and support. This brought about a pantheon with literally hundreds of gods, many of them duplicating each other's particular office, calling for still more involved ceremonies and priesthood.

As communities became more highly organized and the men were relieved to a still greater extent from sharing the labors of the community, an aristocracy arose which was almost on a par with the priesthood. These individuals, being freed from the worrysome labor necessary to support the population, began to find that they had time to think. Under such conditions it was not long before, in each one of the cultural areas of the land, small groups among the higher priests and the leisure class began to realize that, while a multitude of gods were necessary for the agriculturalists and the common people, it was much more likely that there was a single motivating power that kept the world moving smoothly. In Mexico and in Peru the idea of one omnipotent force directing and controlling everything was gaining headway at the time of the Conquest. The intellectual leaders were ready for the preachings of the Spanish priests. It is probably due to this that the wandering friars were tolerated in the newly conquered land. These brave men of God were frequently perplexed by some of the religious ceremonies they found already established in the New World. The general presence of the confessional throughout the major portion of Mexico, baptism as a purification ceremony in

Peru, the use of the cross in Central America, all tended to lead the old padres toward a belief that one of the ancient saints had preached Christianity in the New World in times past. Without a doubt the harsh treatment accorded the priesthood in many parts of the newly conquered land was meted out to them as backsliders. Had there been no resemblance with Christian forms, they would have been treated more gently as out-and-out heathens.

Much of our information regarding the religions in pre-Columbian times has come to us through the journals of the priests who accompanied the Conquistadors, but there are other evidences of the religious beliefs of the primitive people. The methods used in the disposal of the dead are important in this respect. In the early times, that is, in the more primitive cultures, there seems to have been a general fear that the dead might return with evil intent toward the survivors. To thwart such action, the deceased was thoroughly trussed up, for it was supposed that if the arms and legs were bound the spirit too would be bound. This type of burial is equally common in the Old and New Worlds. Later it seems as though this fear of molestation decreased, for trussed and bundled burials disappear. However, the belief that the spirit passed on to another life was still strong, for we see each corpse buried with the utensils it used during life and might need in a life hereafter. Foodstuffs and drink were left with the dead for their use on the journey to their next living place.

The world over such burials have supplied the archeologists with some of the most beautiful examples of
artistic endeavor. I need mention only Tuthankamen's
Tomb and those of Monte Alban in Mexico. The
myriad of little pottery figurines of the goddesses of
fertility that are found in Archaic Mexico have their
counterpart in each of the Old World civilizations. Such
votive offerings have continued to be used to modern
times among the more superstitious peasantry, so we
see that man's religious thought follows along the same
channels wherever he settles.

5

Community organization in the Americas also demon-
strates that there is a uniformity in the way man's mind
works. There arose in the Americas types of government
that are quite familiar to us in the history of our own
European civilization. It is quite probable that the development of civil rule followed the same stages wherever man became established. In some places it advanced more rapidly than in others. Briefly the stages
in the development of the social community will be
outlined and they will apply almost equally in Africa,
Asia, Europe or the Americas.

In the days when man was a nomad, no real work for
the community was possible or necessary. Annual band-
ing together for hunting purposes did occur and it is
possible that a leadership of some sort was present in

those days. When man began to settle down and live in one place, there was at first no community. Each individual selected his own easily defended shelter near the fields he selected to cultivate. It was probably not long before these early farmers learned that their stored produce and their lives would be safer from the marauding nomads if they grouped themselves closer together for mutual protection. This step was the beginning of organized society.

In time certain individuals in the community came to be looked upon as advisors on agricultural problems or in defense of the group. They were consulted on the time to sow and the time to reap, on the best ways of storing the food to be used during the long winter, on the most advantageous methods for defending themselves and their hoarded provender. Before long this led to community chieftainship. For some time such leadership must have been purely elective. However, it was probably noticed that, as a man was relieved from tilling the soil himself, he could be of much more beneficial service to the community as a leader. And thus certain farmers became exempt from contributing brawn and became intellectual guides. We know that in the Old World this was so and that not many generations passed before such an office became hereditary and something like a feudal system grew up. Once a ruling class developed, it was not long before some aristocrat devised a scheme whereby his neighbors joined him in the general defense of the region, and thus the idea of a nation arose.

The ultimate selection of the leader in any nation may be made in either of two ways. His position may be hereditary or it may be elective. It seems that in the Americas both methods were used and that the leader was more frequently elected among the least highly developed groups than among the great cultural divisions. Even today the Pueblos are governed by an elected council of elders quite like that the Spaniards found on their arrival. In Middle and South America the great nations were ruled by hereditary leaders. It is interesting to note here how kinship with the ruling deity was claimed by the ruling family. The divine right of kings seems to be a royal prerogative.

The three great civilizations—the Aztec, the Maya and the Inca—present three philosophies of government. The counterpart of each may be recognized in our European forms of modern times. In the Valley of Mexico the Church and State were synonymous and all-powerful. This was true probably to a great extent in the Maya area. These were typically capitalistic governments that seemed to function quite well. The Aztec system was apparently an autocracy, while that functioning in the Maya area was an oligarchy. In Peru we find quite a different state of affairs. Here there existed for a number of centuries one of the very few successful attempts at a communistic dictatorship. It is interesting in the light of modern communistic thought to see that the plan of government along such lines might be successful but that it demands an absolute dictator at its head. The experiment in Russia during recent years seems to prove this thesis. People as a group never know what is best for themselves. A closer examination of the Inca system of government reveals the smooth functioning of many of the plans that have been suggested for the modification of our own social system. A more thorough study of that ancient American government might be useful to social economists in avoiding the pitfalls that lie before the man who attempts to plan for his neighbor. It is perfectly evident that the pure communism of the Inca period left really little to be desired on the part of the great masses, but it is also evident from the results of the Conquest that it left the people with little or no initiative. All decisions for generations past had been made by the rulers and the mass of the population had no ideas of its own, and thus were exterminated or enslaved in a comparatively short time by a small group of invaders.

Thus we see that at the time of the advent of Europeans into America, the social organizations were democracy, communistic dictatorship, oligarchy and autocracy. Each was subjected to essentially the same type of invasion and the superimposition of an autocracy. Of them only one survives to the present time. The individual independence afforded by the democracy of the Pueblos developed the only group of people capable of withstanding the oppression of the Spaniards.

APPENDIX ONE

DATES OF THE SOUTHWESTERN RUINS DERIVED BY THE TREE RING METHOD

THE unique method of dating the ruins in the Southwest by tree rings has often been described and is easily available to readers through Dr. A. E. Douglass' own article that appeared in *The National Geographic Magazine* for December 1929. Since that time a small corps of workers all trained by Dr. Douglass has been assiduously applying his technique to the timbers and charcoal recovered during the excavation of the ruins. In addition to the master Flagstaff chronology erected by Dr. Douglass and his assistants for the northern Arizona area, Mr. W. S. Stallings, Jr. of the Laboratory for Anthropology at Santa Fe, New Mexico has erected a chronology for the Rio Grande drainage. Mr. Emil Haury of the Gila Pueblo, Globe, Arizona has adapted the Flagstaff chronology to the southern parts of Arizona. Miss Florence Hawley has recently announced a totally independent key to the tree rings of the Tennessee Valley in the east. This last mentioned chronology, when it is verified, will be of utmost importance to the students of the Mound-Builders.

In 1934 the dendrochronologists banded together and began the publication of *The Tree Ring Bulletin*. It is published at Flagstaff, Arizona. Previous to this the dates derived had been published in a number of journals, some of them difficult of access. In order to have available in one place at least an outline of the dates known, I have taken the opportunity to present the dates so far derived in a compact style. I have tried to include all the dates published that are the earliest or latest for the ruins dated. There are some exceptions to this. For instance, twenty-seven Pueblo I–II single room Pit-house ruins from the Flagstaff region are grouped together under one reference 784–1115. All the dates are A. D.

That the information may be of most use to the casual student, the data have been arranged chronologically according to the various drainage systems. The dates given are the earliest and latest that have been deciphered for each ruin. They must not be construed to be limiting. The names appended to a region or to a single date are those of the "tree ringer" or dendrochronologist who has done the deciphering. All the dates were checked by Dr. Douglass previous to their original publication.

Where a range of dates is given, there have been frequently many beams dated within that range, occasionally as many as one hundred. In some cases the earlier dates probably refer to beams that have been re-used. An example of such is a beam from the third story of the Chetro Ketl pueblo in Chaco Canyon, which gives the earliest date in the ruin, fully one hundred years earlier than the probable building date of the room from which it was taken. Dr. Hawley's report on the dating of this ruin is well worth reading to a person interested in the way in which dates are used by archeologists. It will be found in *The University of New Mexico Bulletin Monograph Series* Vol. I, No. 1, 1936.

I want to express here my sincere thanks to Dr. Emil Haury, Mr. John McGregor and especially Mr. W. S. Stallings, Jr. for the invaluable assistance they have given me in assembling this appendix.

SAN JUAN DRAINAGE
Mesa Verde, 612–1274
Dr. A. E. Douglass, Harry T. Getty, Dr. Emil Haury,
W. S. Stallings, Jr. and W. S. Glock

Basket Maker III

612 ±	Step House Earth Lodge (WSG)
625 ±	Step House (WSG)

Pueblo III

1066	Jug House (HTG)
1073–1273	Cliff Palace (AED–HTG)
1086–1106	Lowry Ruin (EH–WSS)
1112–1184	Oak Tree House (AED–HTG)
1115–1143 ± 30	Spring House (AED–HTG)
1177 ± 5	Hemenway House (HTG)
1190–1272	Balcony House (AED–HTG)
1204–1251 ± 5	Square Tower House (AED–HTG)
1216–1274	Spruce Tree House (AED–HTG)
1231 ± 20–1244 ± 20	Long House (HTG)
1261	Number Sixteen House (HTG)
1273	Buzzard House (HTG)

Aztec Region, 1089–1121
Dr. A. E. Douglass

Pueblo III

1089	Solomon Ruin
1110–1121	Aztec Ruin

REDROCK-SHIPROCK REGION, 354–857

W. S. Glock

Basket Maker III

354, 490–692	Broken Flute Cave
477–486	Obelisk Cave
533	Black Horse Creek Cave 6
630, 642–759	Black Horse Creek Caves 1, 2, 6, 7, 8
675, 795–857	Morris' site on Bennet's Peak

CHACO CANYON, 777–1130

Dr. A. E. Douglass and Dr. F. M. Hawley

Pueblo I–II

777	Judd's Pit-house in the wash (AED)

Pueblo II–III

857 ± 10–1063 ± 15	Una Vida (FMH)
859–1130	Pueblo Bonito (AED)
898–1087	Peñasco Blanco (AED–FMH)
941–1124	Kinbinola (FMH–AED)
942–1087	Hungo Pavi (AED–FMH)
945–1116	Chetro Ketl (FMH–AED)
	The following dates from the Chetro Ketl complex may be of interest:
	1069–1130 Kivas A, G, H, I, J, K (FMH)
	1024–1078 Talus site I (FMH)
	1101 Talus Rock Shelter (FMH)
1053–1103	Pueblo del Arroyo (AED)
1060	Pueblo Pintado (FMH)
1084	Kinklizin (FMH)

1106	Kinya-A (FMH)
1111	Tsinklitsin (FMH)
1123	Yellow House (AED) also called Kinklitzo

CANYON DE CHELLY, 348–1284

Dr. A. E. Douglass, W. S. Glock, Alfred Peterson

Basket Maker III

| 348–702 | Mummy Cave (WSG) |
| 701–787 | Canyon del Muerto Cave I (WSG) |

Pueblo II

| 936–957, 1284? | Sliding Ruin (AP–AED) |

Pueblo III

| 1060–1275 | White House Pueblo (AED–AP) |
| 1253–1284 | Mummy Cave (AED) |

TSEGI CANYON, 980–1286

Dr. A. E. Douglass and John McGregor

Pottery from all but first three sites: Kayenta Black-on-White and Polychrome, Tusayan Polychrome

980 ± 6	Turkey House (JM)
1018	unnamed ruin N.A. 2543 (JM)
1064 ± 5–1067 ± 10	Ladder House (JM)
1116 ± 10–1286	Kiet Siel—Keetseel (AED–JM)
1124–1130 ± 3	unnamed ruin N.A. 2630 (JM)
1208 ± 3–1280 ± 2	Twin Cave Pueblo (JM)
1242–1286	Betatakin (AED)
1274	Calamity Cave (JM)

1275	Bat Woman House (JM)
1275	unnamed ruin N.A. 2606 near Loloma Ki (JM)
1278	Loloma Ki (JM)
1286	Rubbish Ruin (AED)

UTAH REGION, 1133–1244

Dr. A. E. Douglass and W. S. Stallings, Jr.

Pueblo III

1133–1135	Grand Gulch Ruin (AED)
1243–1244	Five Kiva House (WSS)

LITTLE COLORADO DRAINAGE
NAVAJO DESERT REGION, 1112–1804

Dr. A. E. Douglass

Pueblo III and historic

1112–1126	Klag-E-Toh
1126–1130	Red House—Kin-Kle-Chee
1255–1285	Wide and Butterfly Ruins, Kivas—Kintiel
1720–1804	Kinnazinde

ZUÑI REGION, 844–1480

Dr. A. E. Douglass and Carl Miller, Jr.

Pueblo I–II

844–918	Allentown House A–I Pueblo I (CM)
858–886	Allentown House 4/34 " I (CM)

1011 ± 2   Allentown Kiva 32/G   Pueblo II (CM)

Pueblo IV

1381–1480   Hamikuh (AED)

JEDITO-HOPI PLATEAU REGION, 941 TO DATE

Dr. A. E. Douglass and Alfred Peterson

1119   Kiminiloa (AP)
1217–1495   Kawaiku (AED)
1255–1269 &
1369–1430   Kokopnyama (AED)
1370–1800   Oraibi (AED–AP) now inhabited by Hopi
1377–1390   Chakpahu (AED)
1390–1800   Shongopovi (AED–AP) now inhabited by Hopi
1427–1605   Walpi (AED) now inhabited by Hopi
1435–1614   Sichomovi (AED) now inhabited by Hopi
1557–1590   Shipaulovi (AED–AP) now inhabited by Hopi

FLAGSTAFF REGION, 680–1381

Dr. A. E. Douglass and John McGregor

Pueblo I–II

680–1115   Range of dates for 27 pit-houses in the region near Sunset Crater. Most of the dates by JM. The change from Pueblo I to Pueblo II took place about 875

1276	Latest date for a pit-house (JM)
888–1094	Walnut Canyon Cliff Dwelling (JM)
904–1060	Medicine Fort Ruin (JM)

Pueblo III

Pottery—Flagstaff Black-on-White, Tusayan Polychrome, Verde Black-on-Gray

1073–1205	Wupatki (AED)
1168–1278	Turkey Hill Pueblo (AED)
1183	Nalalihu (JM) at the foot of Citadel Ruin
1192	Fewkes Ruin (AED)
1192–1260	Citadel Ruin (AED)
1381	Chaves Pass Ruin (AED)

MOGOLLON MESA AND SOUTHERN ARIZONA,
896–1385
Dr. A. E. Douglass and Dr. Emil Haury

896–908	Type village of Mogollon Culture (EH)
1132–1231	Pinedale, Pueblo III, St. John Polychrome pottery (AED–EH)
1170–1205	Tusayan Kivas, Pueblo III (AED–EH)
1174–1272	Showlow, Pueblo III (AED–EH) Early occupation
1248–1348	Range of dates from 13 cliff dwellings in the Sierra Ancha—all Pueblo IV (EH)
1293–1330	Pinedale, Pueblo III, Pinedale polychrome pottery (AED–EH)

1356–1383	Showlow, Pueblo IV (AED–EH) Late occupation
1345	Gila Pueblo, Room 90, Pueblo IV (EH)
1385	Gila Pueblo, Room 98, Pueblo IV (EH)

RIO GRANDE AND PECOS DRAINAGE, 1310–1657

W. S. Stallings, Jr.

Pueblo III

1310 ± 5	Water Canyon Ridge Ruin, Pajarito; Pottery—Santa Fe Black-on-White
1310 ± 5	unnamed site, LA309, a site in the Galisteo basin about 2½ miles north of San Cristobal; Pottery—Santa Fe and Galisteo Black-on-White
$1275 + X$ (est. 1300 ± 10)	unnamed site near Lamy LA27; Pottery—Santa Fe and Galisteo Black-on-White
1335–1336	Riana Ruin; Pottery—Santa Fe Black-on-White

Pueblo IV

$1331 + X$ (est. 1375 ± 25)	Posi—Poseuinge; Biscuit ware, A and B
$1320 + X$ (est. 1375 ± 25)	Hupobi—Homayo; Biscuit ware, A and B
1348–1612	Pecos Ruin (site abandoned in 1838); Pottery—Black-on-White, glaze-paint and modern dull paint wares

1349 ± 2–1366	Armstrong Ruin, Gallo Canyon; Pottery—Chupadero Black-on-White, Glaze I and many trade wares
1390	Glorietta Ruin; Pottery—Black-on-White, Glaze I
1427–1442 ± 5	San Cristobal (Room X of N. C. Nelson); Pottery—Glaze-paint
1430s & 1440s	Building period of South House Pecos Ruin; Pottery—Glaze II
1431–1490 ± 5	Tunque; Pottery—Glazed ware
1435	Pueblo Largo of N. C. Nelson; Pottery—Glazed ware
1447	Frijolito; Pottery—largely Glaze IV with earlier and later types
1440 + X (est. 1460 ± 15)	Tyuonyi; Pottery—largely Glaze IV with earlier and later types
1460 + X (est. 1480 ± 10) to 1574	Tshirege; Pottery—Biscuit ware and Sankawi Black-on-Cream
1507–1565 ± 3	Puyé; Pottery—largely Glaze IV with earlier and later types represented
1572–1594	Unshagi; Pottery—Jemez Black-on-White and late Glaze wares
1657	Large unnamed Jemez ruin, LA136, between Vallecito Viejo and San Juan Canyon, Rio Jemez drainage; Pottery—late Glazed wares

MAYA DATES EXPRESSED IN THE CHRISTIAN CHRONOLOGY ACCORDING TO THE MORLEY AND THE GOODMAN CORRELATIONS

Maya Dates	Place of Inscription	(2)	According to Morley	According to Goodman	Reference (1)
8.6.2–4–17	Tuxtla Statu-ette	—	98.906 B. C.	162.021 A. D.	M, p. 411
8.14.3–1–12	Leyden Plate	—	55.500 A. D.	314.615	
8.14.10–13–15	Uaxactun, Stela 9	E	63.117	322.232	
9.0.10–0–0 ?	Tikal, Stela 8	(E)	186.641	445.756	
* 9.1.10–0–0 ?	Copan, Stela 20	(E)	206.354	465.469	
9.2.10–0–0	Copan, Stela 24	E	226.067	485.182	M
9.2.13–0–0	Tikal, Stela 3	E	228.972	488.087	M
9.3.0–0–0	Uaxactun	E	235.924	495.039	G
9.5.5–0–0 ??	Piedras Neg-ras, Stela 29	(E)	280.278	539.393	M
9.6.0–0–0	Tonina	E	295.063	554.178	G
† 9.6.10–0–0	Tuluum, Stela 1	—	304.919	564.034	See footnote
9.7.0–0–0	Pusilhá	E	314.776	573.891	G
9.8.15–0–0	Piedras Neg-ras, Stela 25	E	349.273	608.388	M
9.10.0–0–0	Naranjo, Lin-tel	E	373.915	633.030	M
	El Pabellón, Stela 1	E			M
9.10.5–0–0 ??	Altar de Sacri-ficios, Stela 5	(E)	378.843	627.958	M
* 9.10.10–0–0	Altar de Sacri-ficios, Stela 4	(E)	383.771	642.886	

Maya Dates	Place of Inscription (2)		According to Morley	According to Goodman	Reference (1)
	Palenque, Temple of the Sun	E			
9.10.19–13–0	Copan, "Sundial" Stelae 10 & 12		393.371	652.486	
9.11.5–0–0 ?	Yaxha, Stela 6	—	398.556	657.671	
9.13.0–0–0	Tzendales, Temple of the Tablet	—	433.054	692.169	
9.14.0–0–0	Altar de Sacrificios, Stela 7	L	452.767	711.882	
??	Itsimte, Altar I	(E)			
	Xultun	E			G
9.14.10–0–0	Itsimte, Altar 2	E	462.623	721.738	M
* 9.15.0–0–0	Pusilhá	L	472.480	731.595	G
	Quirigua	E			G
9.15.10–0–0	Itsimte, Stela 2	L	482.336	741.451	
9.15.15–0–0	Yaxchilan, Altar	E	487.264	746.379	M
	Quirigua, Stela S	E			M
9.16.0–0–0	Seibal, Stairway	E	492.193	751.308	M
9.16.10–0–0 ??	La Honradez, Stela 6	(E)	502.049	761.164	M
9.17.0–0–0	La Honradez, Stela 7	E	511.906	771.021	
	Nakun, Stela U	E			
9.17.5–0–0	El Cayo	—	516.834	775.949	G
9.17.10–0–0 ?	Ixkun, Stela 2	(E)	521.762	780.877	M
	Los Higos, Stela 1	—			
	Chinkultic	E			G
9.17.15–0–0	La Mar	E	526.690	785.805	G
9.18.0–0–0	Aguas Calientes, Stela 1	E	531.619	790.734	

Maya Dates	Place of Inscription	(2)	According to Morley	According to Goodman	Reference (1)
	Cancuen, Stela 2	E			
	Ixkun, Stela 1	E			
9.18.5–0–0	Cancuen, Altar 2	L	536.547	795.662	
	Piedras Negras, Stela 12	L			
9.18.10–0–0	Copan, Altar G_1	L	541.475	800.590	
?	La Honradez, Stela 4	L			
?	Ixkun, Stela 5	L			M
9.18.15–0–0	La Mar, Stela 2	L	546.403	805.518	
9.19.0–0–0	Tonina	L	551.332	810.447	G
	Quirigua, Temple I	L			
	Uaxactun, Stela 7	L			M
	Hatzcap Ceel	E			G
9.19.10–0–0	Naranjo, Stela 32	L	561.188	820.303	M
10.0.5–0–0	Hatzcap Ceel	L	575.973	835.088	G
10.0.15–0–0	Chinkultic	L	585.829	844.944	G
10.1.0–0–0	Benque Viejo, Stela 1	—	590.758	849.873	
	Flores, Stela 2	E			
	Nakum, Stela D	L			
	Ucanal, Stela 3	—			
10.2.0–0–0	Flores, Stela 1	L	610.471	869.586	M
	Seibal, Stela 1	L			
	Tikal, Stela 11	L			
10.2.5–0–0	Quen Santo, Stela 1	E	615.399	874.514	
10.2.10–0–0	Quen Santo, Stela 2	L	620.327	879.442	
	Chichen Itza, Temple of				

Maya Dates	Place of Inscription	(2)	According to Morley	According to Goodman	Reference (1)
	Initial Series	—			
10.3.0–0–0	Uaxactun	L	630.184	889.299	G
	Xultun	L			G
10.6.10–0–0 ?	Tuluum, Stela 1	—	699.176	958.294	M
‡ 11.12.8–13–4	Chichen Itza, Cena Principal		1210.418	1469.533	M, p. 520
‡ 11.12.17–11–1	Uxmal, Monjas	—	1217.451	1476.566	M, p. 514
‡ 11.15.16–12–14	Uxmal, Ball Court	—	1277.391	1536.506	M, p. 515
‡ 11.19.11–0–0	Chichen Itza, High Priest's Grave		1350.676	1609.791	M, p. 518

(1) M—Morley, S. G., The Inscriptions at Copan, Appendix VIII, 1920

G—Gann, Thos., History of the Maya (with Eric Thompson), Chapter II, 1931

When no reference is given, the date is to be found in both books.

(2) E—Earliest date

L—Latest date

( )—Parenthesis denotes uncertain dates.

Dr. Morley's correlation dates are derived from his tables on pp. 504, 505, etc. The Goodman dates were computed by the present author, using the data set forth by Dr. John Teeple in *Contribution to American Archeology*, Vol. I, No. 2, Carnegie Institution, 1931.

* These dates as given by Dr. Gann differ from those of Dr. Morley used above:

Copan, Stela 20 given as 9.1.0–0–0, 195 A. D.

Altar de Sacrificios, Stela 4 given as 9.10.0–0–0, 373 A. D.

Pusilhá, 9.15.0–0–0 transcribes to 472 not 371 as given by Dr. Gann.

Many other dates given by Dr. Gann differ from those given by Dr. Morley by one year.

† According to Dr. Morley this is not the contemporaneous date for Tuluum, Stela 1. Both 9.6.10–0–0 and 10.6.10–0–0 are on the stone. Morley accepts the last date as contemporaneous with its erection.

‡ These dates have been derived by Dr. Morley from *katun*-ending dates and are probably true but there is some uncertainty.

?—Dr. Morley considers the transcription of the glyphs very doubtful.

APPENDIX THREE

A SHORT SELECTED BIBLIOGRAPHY

THIS volume has been planned with two ends in view: to arouse an interest in American archeology and to present some of the problems that confront us by skipping through the great volume of material that has been accumulated by others, touching only those points that are of general interest; to stimulate the desire for further reading in the field by students of American history and just interested readers. The following list of books has been selected to help fulfill the second aim. It is in no way complete and possibly I have omitted some of the best books. These I suggest because I found them distinctly readable.

Ancient Man

Hooton, E. A.—Up from the Ape—Macmillan
Probably the best recent summary of what we know of man and his ancestors from a physiological and anatomical point of view.

Osborn, H. F.—Men of the Old Stone Age—Scribners
The history of man from the time he first worked in stone until he turned to metals. Confined to the discoveries in Europe. Well illustrated and good reading.

Keith, Sir Arthur—The Antiquity of Man, 2 vol.—Lippincott—New Discoveries relating to the Antiquity of Man—Norton
Rather technical but by far the most informative vol-

umes on the subject. All discoveries of ancient man are discussed.

The four following scientific papers are suggested for a good picture of the status of ancient man in the Southwest at the time of this writing:

Harrington, M. R.—Southwest Museum Papers, no. 8, 1933, Los Angeles
The results of the excavation of Gypsum Cave, Nevada.

Howard, E. B.—Museum Journal, Vol. 24, no. 2–3, 1935, University of Pennsylvania Museum
The evidence of early man in North America.

Roberts, F. H. H., Jr.—Smithsonian Miscellaneous Collections, Vol. 94, no. 4, 1935 and Vol. 95, no. 10, 1936
Reports on the Lindenmeier site of Folsom material. Additional reports on this site will follow in the same publication.

The Southwest

Hewett, E. L.—Ancient Life in the American Southwest—Bobbs-Merrill
The only complete popular summary of the archeology and anthropology of the Pueblo region.

Kidder, A. V.—Southwest Archeology—Yale—1924
A report on the Andover excavations at Pecos and a most excellent summary of Southwest pottery. Out of print and hard to get. No. 1 of the series noted at the close of this bibliography.

Mexico

Biart, L.—The Aztecs—A. C. McClurg & Co.
The only popular book devoted solely to these people.

It is translated from the French and is out of date but still the only thing available.

Blum, F.—The Conquest of Yucatan—Houghton Mifflin
To date the most complete summary of the history of the Maya in Yucatan.

Gann, T. and Thompson, J. E.—The History of the Maya— Scribner
A brief but fairly comprehensive treatment of the history of the entire Maya Empire.

Spinden, H.—Ancient Civilizations in Mexico and Central America—American Museum of Natural History
A brief guide to the cultures of Mexico.

Thompson, J. E.—Mexico before Cortez—Scribner
The best popular summary of ancient life in Mexico.

Thompson, J. E.—The Civilization of the Mayas—Scribner

South America

Means, P. A.—The Ancient Civilizations of the Andes— Scribner
The only volume available that does justice to the subject.

Mound-Builders

Shetrone, H. C.—The Mound-Builders—Appleton
The first real attempt to bring order out of the chaotic mass of material published on these ancient people.

More Technical Sources of Information

Publications of: The American Museum of Natural History
The Bureau of Ethnology
University of California
The Carnegie Institution

University of Chicago
The Heye Foundation: Museum of the
American Indian
Peabody Museum at Cambridge
University of Pennsylvania
Tulane University

Craft Techniques

Kissell, M. L.—Basketry of the Papago and Pima—American
Museum of Natural History

Roberts, H. H.—Basketry of the San Carlos Apache—American Museum of Natural History

These three volumes form a splendid picture of the development of basketry in the southwestern part of the United States from the prehistoric to modern times.

Weltfish, G.—Preliminary Classification of pre-Historic South Western Basketry—Smithsonian

Guthe, C. E.—Pueblo Pottery Making—Yale—1925, no. 2 of Pecos Series

Kidder, A. V.—Pecos Pottery—2 vol. Yale.—1931, 1936, no. 5 & 7 of Pecos Series, Vol. 1 with C. A. Amsden; Vol. 2 with A. O. Sheppard

These three volumes are the most important recent works on Pueblo pottery. They are somewhat technical but are not too difficult to read and understand. They are an ideal starting point for a deeper study of this craft in the Southwest.

Kidder, A. V.—The Artifacts of Pecos—Yale—1932, no. 6 of Pecos Series

NOTE: Two other volumes have been published in conjunction with the five noted above based on the Pecos Excavations undertaken by Dr. Kidder for the Robert S.

Peabody Foundation for Archeology, Phillips Academy, Andover, N. H. These are:

No. 3. The Pueblo of Jemez—E. C. Parson, 1925

No. 4. The Indians of Pecos Pueblo—E. A. Hooton, 1930

An eighth volume on the excavation of the pueblo is in preparation. This series when completed will constitute the most thorough study ever made in the Pueblo area and should serve as a guide to future workers both in their excavation and in the preparation of their reports.

Appendix Four

THE AMERICAN TIME-TABLE.

	THE PUEBLO AREA		THE MEXICAN AREA	
B.C. A.D.	We know nothing about these early times	T H E B A S K E T M A K E R S	The ARCHAIC PERIOD about which we know very little	
500	New people arriving from the east established the Mogollon culture		IF the great Pedrogal lava flow occured at about the same time as Sunset Crater erupted then this culture was at its peak in the 8th century	
	The Early Pueblo culture was well es- tablished in northern Arizona	Sunset Crater erupted about 885		T H E T O L T E C S
1000	The Golden Age opened	T H E P U E B L O S	The Toltecs hired out as mercenaries to Mayapan	
	Mesa Verde well populated		Quetzalcoatl introduced the calendar system 1123	
	The Golden Age closed with the Great Draught 1276 to 1299		The Nahual invasion began 1220	
1500			Acamapichtli was "emperor" 1376	A Z T E C S
	The Spaniards arrived 1540		The Spaniards were victor- ious, 1521	

THE MAYAN AREA		THE ANDEAN AREA		
Archaic Period of Migration		A Period of Migration		
		On the coast the Early Chimu and Nazca cultures developed and expanded. In the mountains the Tiahuanaco I culture developed on the shores of Lake Titicaca.	C H I M U N A Z C A & T I A H U A N	B.C. A.D. — — — — 500 —
The Mayan people settled in the forests of Peten and developed their great architecture	T H E O L D E M P I R E			
		The mountaineers began to invade the coastal regions.		
9.15.0-0-0, The Great Period began and in The migration to Yucatan began closed 10.2.-0-0		The Tiahuanaco II Empire established. The coastal civiliz- ations subject to the mountain people.	T I A H U A N A C O	—
The League of Mayapan The Toltecs hired in Katun 2 Ahau	T H E	The coastal valleys threw off the rule of Tiahuanaco	The Empire declined II	1000
The Toltecs gained dom- inance, the end of the League. Katun 8 Ahau	N E W	The Late Chimu and Nazca rules on the coast	C N H A I Z M C U A	—
The Toltecs lost out to the Xiu. Katun 8 Ahau	E M P I R E	The Incas arose in Cuzco and the coast again fell under the rule of mountaineers	I N	— 1500
Yucatan conquered by the Spaniards 1542 Katun 11 Ahau		The Spaniards arrived 1530	C A S	

INDEX

ALSO BY LAURA CLARIDGE

Emily Post: Daughter of the Gilded Age,
Mistress of American Manners

Norman Rockwell: A Life

Tamara de Lempicka: A Life of Deco and Decadence

Romantic Potency: The Paradox of Desire

Out of Bounds: Male Writers and Gender(ed) Criticism (coeditor)